BOOKS BY ROBERT L. ROWAN AND PAUL J. GILLETTE

Your Prostate
The Gay Health Guide

THE GAY HEALTH GUIDE

THE GAY HEALTH GUIDE

A Modern Medicine Book

ROBERT L. ROWAN, M.D.

PAUL J. GILLETTE, PH.D.

LITTLE, BROWN AND COMPANY
Boston • Toronto

FIRST EDITION

T 05/78

LIBRARY OF CONGRESS CATALOGING IN PUBLICATION DATA

Rowan, Robert L
  The gay health guide.

  (A modern medicine book)
  Includes index.
  1. Homosexuals — Health and hygiene. 2. Hygiene,
Sexual. 3. Venereal diseases — Prevention.
4. Homosexuality — United States — Societies, etc. —
Directories. I. Gillette, Paul J., joint author.
II. Title.
RA788.R66   613.9'5   78-766
ISBN 0-316-31356-4

Designed by Janis Capone

*Published simultaneously in Canada
by Little, Brown & Company (Canada) Limited*

PRINTED IN THE UNITED STATES OF AMERICA

Contents

THE GAY HEALTH
GUIDE

Introduction

This is a book about minimizing the health hazards of homosexual activity. They are many and serious.

The fact is, the typical homosexually active male will get venereal disease ten times more often than the typical male whose activity is exclusively heterosexual. The typical homosexually active female, owing mainly to anatomical factors, will get V.D. much less often, but is nonetheless susceptible.

Even if you don't get V.D. — defined as sexually transmitted infection — you may suffer one of many other physical problems. They range from the merely inconvenient, such as infestation by parasitic insects, to the severely limiting, such as fecal incontinence resulting from irreversible stretching of the anal sphincter muscle. They include, chiefly among males, rupture of the walls of the rectum and possibly fatal infection of the abdominal cavity; chiefly among females, misdiagnosis of venereal or other serious diseases because a physician learns that a woman has no heterosexual contacts and wrongly assumes that she is also homosexually inactive.

The point here is that by knowing what can happen and the circumstances under which these things are likely to happen, you can reduce the chances of their happening to you. Also, by recognizing them when they do happen, you can minimize many of their effects and protect your partner(s) from similar problems.

This book is for homosexually active people and for others who, though not active at present, desire homosexual relationships but fear the health consequences. It is also for husbands and wives of homosexually active people who may be concerned about these persons' health risks and about the very real possibility of catching a disease from them. Finally, it is for the parents, children, spouses, and other relatives and friends of homosexually active people who wish to know more about homosexuality in general.

Some people experience anxiety related to homosexuality, either because they are active and believe they should not be or because they desire activity but feel compelled to abstain. Some wonder — along with their parents, spouses, children, other relatives, or friends — if it is possible to overcome homosexual desire and convert to a life of exclusive heterosexuality. These are interesting and important matters, and we shall offer our thoughts on them later in the book, but they are not health matters. Homosexuality is not an illness. By definition, behavior or states of appetite cannot be illnesses. At the very most, they can be symptoms. There is no convincing evidence at present that homosexual appetite or behavior is symptomatic of anything. Whatever problems they may engender are not health problems.

Why is this distinction between health and nonhealth so important? Because only if a problem is defined accurately can it be understood, and only if it is understood can it be solved. Life is complicated enough without adding the confusion of metaphors masquerading as facts.

CHAPTER 1

Venereal Diseases

Today, almost four decades after the wonder-drug penicillin promised to eradicate the most serious venereal diseases, these same diseases are more widespread than ever. Another major and sometimes fatal disease, hepatitis B, previously not considered likely to be transmitted sexually, has recently become epidemic among homosexually active males. More than a dozen lesser infections — lesser in terms of the damage they do, not the number of people they afflict — are far more prevalent among people who have many sex partners than among people having few partners.

The number and variety of diseases that can be transmitted sexually have persuaded medical scientists to revise their original concept of venereal disease. Half a century ago, the adjective was applied to only five diseases — syphilis, gonorrhea, chancroid, lymphogranuloma venereum, and granuloma inguinale. It was believed that these were the only diseases that were transmitted sexually, and that they could not be transmitted any other way.

Both beliefs proved erroneous. It is true that the organisms that carry these diseases thrive in the human genitals and cannot survive for longer than a few seconds except on a moist human surface. Thus, nonhuman animals neither contract nor transmit the diseases, and you can't get them from a toilet seat (except in the extremely unlikely situation where a previous occupant deposited infectious moisture on the seat and you touched it with a moist surface of your body before the organism could die). However, in certain situations, transmission may be nonsexual. Dentists have contracted syphilis by touching a chancre in a patient's mouth. Gonorrhea has been transmitted on the hands from an infected person's penis to someone else's eyes. Babies may acquire either of these diseases or others from the mother during or shortly after birth.

While physicians were discovering that the so-called venereal diseases could be transmitted nonvenereally, they also were learning that other diseases, previously considered nonvenereal, could be spread by sexual contact. Of course, many infections can be transmitted by general exposure to a carrier. These include tuberculosis, typhoid fever, influenza, smallpox, measles, and pneumonia. Not surprisingly, if the infectious organism can travel through the air or on the saliva or hands or clothing, sexual contact will often result in infection. However, there are many other diseases in which sexual contact is far more likely to produce infection than general nonsexual contact. The Center for Disease Control, U. S. Public Health Service, calculates that there are at least eighteen diseases (including syphilis and the other four original "venereals") that are transmitted *principally* during sexual contact. Current medical practice is to consider all eighteen venereal and to use the terms "venereal disease" (or "V.D.") and "sexually transmitted disease" interchangeably.

Contrary to popular rumor, not all V.D. is curable with a shot of penicillin. There are two sexually transmitted diseases — hepatitis B/genital, also known as "serum hepatitis" or "Australia antigen hepatitis," and herpes simplex type I — that have no known effective treatment. Some victims of hepatitis recover on their own with no permanent effects; others suffer permanent liver damage or die. Herpes appears to be harmless in adults but can cause nerve damage or death in a fetus that contracts the infection from the mother. Herpes has also been linked — though not definitively — with cancer in adults.

The other serious venereal diseases, fortunately, do respond to penicillin or broad-spectrum antibiotics. However, many people acquire V.D. without symptoms; the disease may go undetected until serious damage is done. If a pregnant woman has any undetected venereal disease, even though she herself suffers no damage, the infection may injure or kill the fetus.

One of the main reasons venereal infection proliferates so rapidly is that an asymptomatic carrier may infect hundreds of people before the disease is discovered. Each of these hundreds may go on to infect hundreds of others. Even when symptoms appear, there is an incubation period of several days to several weeks. A person can — and generally will — infect other partners during this period.

Some people will continue to have sex even after symptoms have appeared. Many do not recognize the symptoms. Among those who do, some do not realize the disease is infectious. Shortly before he began working on this book, Robert Rowan treated a young man for syphilis. The man said he had had only one partner during the past several months. Rowan asked his patient to telephone the partner immediately and warn him not to have sex with anyone else before he got treatment.

"Jack," said the patient on the phone, "I'm at the doctor's office, and he says I have syphilis."

"That's really too bad. There must be a lot of it going around," came the reply. "I've had a case for months."

Among people who know the disease is contagious, some persuade themselves there is only a slim possibility of infecting a partner. (Actually, there is a strong probability that the partner will be infected.) A small number go ahead and have sex even though they believe the partner will be infected. "I just couldn't pass up the opportunity, he was too gorgeous," a patient once told Rowan. "At my age, it's not often you get a chance with someone that attractive."

Statistically, homosexually active men have many more partners in a given year than the typical man whose activity is exclusively heterosexual; many homosexually active women have more partners than the typical woman whose activity is exclusively heterosexual. In other words, the mere fact that you are homosexually active exposes you to greater risk of V.D. than the person whose activity is exclusively heterosexual because your partner, if not also you yourself, is likely to have had more opportunities to contract a venereal disease.

Add the element of geography: you are much more likely to contract V.D. in major metropolitan areas than in small towns.

(More than 50 percent of the two million Americans who contract gonorrhea in a given year live in metropolitan areas; these areas hold less than 25 percent of the nation's population.) Homosexually active people tend to live in metropolitan areas because, among other reasons, they tend to suffer less discrimination there and have greater opportunities to meet people of similar inclination. Add another multiplier to the incidence of V.D. among homosexually active people.

And add the element of age: more than half the people who contract venereal disease in a given year are under twenty-five. In some urban areas, 10 to 25 percent of the entire under-twenty-five population is infected. Homosexual activity, and especially multiparty activity, involves a disproportionate number of people under twenty-five.

In many public health clinics, more people who seek treatment for V.D. report that they were infected homosexually than report they were infected heterosexually. While statistics compiled among physicians in private practice are neither as extensive nor reliable, these figures also suggest a disproportionate prevalence of V.D. among the homosexually active. How this state of affairs came about is irrelevant; the fact remains, if you have only *one* sexual contact — *ever* — you are statistically more likely to get V.D. homosexually than heterosexually.

Let us now examine the various venereal diseases. In discussing each, we will answer the questions, What is it? How do you get it? How do you know you have it? How is it diagnosed? How is it treated? How can you avoid it?

Many physicians diagnose and treat venereal diseases improperly because of a lack of familiarity with these diseases. The most common treatment error is the underprescribing of drugs, caution in this instance being more harmful than helpful. Physicians are urged, therefore, to contact the Venereal Disease Control Division of the Center for Disease Control, Atlanta, Georgia 30333, for the most current information on treatment schedules. These schedules are formulated by a committee of distinguished academic and clinical venereologists and are continuously revised as new advances are made in the treatment of venereal disease.

CHAPTER 2

Syphilis

(Transmitted Homosexually among Men and Women)

You wake with a sore on your genitals or your mouth. You think it may be a simple cold sore. Or perhaps you burned yourself with a cigarette or caught your flesh in a zipper. You don't remember any of this happening, but it must have. What else could it be?

If you ignore the sore, it will go away. A small scar may remain, but it usually won't be visible. You conclude that, however you got the sore, everything is okay now.

It isn't. About six weeks later you get a rash that neither burns nor itches. You may get a sore throat, hoarseness, swollen glands in the neck and armpits, warts on or near the genitals, a low, persisting fever, constant headaches that intensify at night, nausea, constipation, pain in the long bones, and/or loss of appetite. In rare cases, hair may start to fall out in clusters.

You tell yourself it's the flu, you take some aspirin, and you go to bed. You feel lousy for a few days, then you improve. After a week or two you feel fine.

You're not. You have syphilis. You've just gone through the primary and secondary stages. A tertiary stage may begin anywhere from three to forty years later. In some people, the disease will attack the heart and major blood vessels, eventually causing death. In other cases, the spinal cord and brain will be affected, sometimes fatally. In still other cases there are no further symptoms. But you still have syphilis, and you'll have it for the rest of your life.

What is it?

Syphilis is the most dangerous of the sexually transmitted diseases. It can attack and destroy almost any organ or body

9

system: the liver, lungs, stomach, nerves, muscles, bones. It can cause paralysis, blindness, insanity. Indeed, it sounds like the nightmare-come-true that they used to tell you would happen if you masturbated. Everything but hair on your palms.

The name "Syphilis" dates to the sixteenth century and the Italian poet-physician Girolamo Fracastoro, who wrote under the name "Fracastor." In 1530 he published the poem *Syphilis, sive Morbus Gallicus* ("Syphilis, or the French Disease"), in which a Hispanic shepherd named Syphilis is struck with disease by vengeful gods as a punishment for blasphemy. Among his burdens, his name would thenceforth be associated with the malady with which he had been smitten. The disease was epidemic in Europe at that time.

In a more scientific work, *Contagion*, published fifteen years later, Fracastor noted that some of his contemporaries theorized that the crew of Christopher Columbus brought syphilis to Europe from the New World. He argued that this was unlikely, since outbreaks were reported simultaneously in Spain, France, Germany, Italy, and Russia — too broad a territory to be covered in a short time by the returning sailors or those they might infect. Fracastor chose to leave open the question of where the original germ gestated. Meanwhile, other Europeans were quick to blame neighboring countries. The English physician John Astruc, in *A Treatise of Venereal Disease*, published at London in 1754, notes:

> ... the Neapolitans and the rest of the Italians called it the French Disease, *Mal Francese*, alleging it was imported into Italy by the French when they attacked the Kingdom of Naples in the year 1494; while the French, on the contrary, called it the Neapolitan or Italian Disease, *Mal de Naples*, because it was first catched by them in the Kingdom of Naples during the above mentioned Expedition: the Germans, too, called it *Frantzozen*, or *Frantzozischen Pocken*, that is, the French Disease or the French Pox; and the English likewise called it by the same Name, because it was propagated in those different nations by the French. ... It was called by the Flemish and Dutch, *Spaanse Pocken*; by the Portuguese, the Castilian Disease; by the East-Indians and Japanese, The Disease of the Portuguese ... by the Persians, The Disease of the Turks; by the Polanders, the Disease of

the Germans; and last of all, by the Russians, the Disease of the Po-landers. . . .

Chauvinistic buck-passing aside, there is no convincing evidence of where syphilis originated. For centuries the disease has been found throughout the world. The germ that causes it — the microbacterium spirochete, treponema pallidum — was identified in 1905 by the German physician Fritz R. Schaudinn.

He must have had exceptional eyesight. The spirochete is so delicate that the ordinary light of a microscope passes right through it. It is so small that it is measured in microns. A micron represents a distance of 10^{-3} millimeters. When none of Schaudinn's colleagues could see the treponema pallidum through an ordinary microscope, he invented a special instrument: the dark-field microscope, which provides a dark background against which a specimen might be viewed.

A year later, the German physician Augusta Paul von Wasserman developed the blood test still in use to demonstrate the presence of syphilis, and three years after that, German histologist Paul Ehrlich developed the first effective treatment for the disease.

Ehrlich's treatment involved a compound containing a strong dose of the poison arsenic. The compound, Salvarsan, worked like, in Ehrlich's term, a "magic bullet" that killed the syphilis germs without damaging the rest of the body. Ehrlich, who only a year earlier had been awarded the Nobel Prize for his work in immunology, was hailed as the father of the modern era of chemotherapy.

Unfortunately, his "magic bullet" occasionally misfired. Many patients experienced serious side effects. Some died. Still, the Salvarsan treatment was the only one that offered any hope of conquering syphilis. That remained true until 1943, when penicillin, which had been discovered eight years earlier, first was used specifically for syphilis.

Large-scale research was not undertaken until after a substantial number of syphilis victims were cured serendipitously while being treated with penicillin for other diseases. The general attitude seems to have been that infected people brought their problems on themselves (by doing this dirty and immoral thing), so let them rot. While the attitude has been modified somewhat in recent years, a continuing antisexual bias remains. If one did not exist, syphilis might have been eradicated long ago.

How do you get it?

You get syphilis through contact with someone who has it. That contact need not be sexual: dentists can get it from a patient and babies can get it from a mother. But in the overwhelming majority of cases, contact is sexual.

Sexual does not necessarily mean genital. The treponema pallidum can survive in any moist and warm human environment. Its preferred habitat during the primary stage of syphilis is the genitals, but it also inhabits the anus and mouth. In a few cases (the dentist's among them) direct contact with a chancre will transmit infection to a surface that is not naturally moist: a finger, for example. But usually there must be contact between two moist surfaces. That means any combination involving the mouth, anus, and genitals (while the surface of the uncircumcised penis is not naturally moist, it becomes moistened during contact with the mouth, anus, or vagina; meanwhile, the urethra, or urinary passageway, is naturally moist).

Prolonged contact is not necessary. The longer contact lasts, the greater the opportunity for large numbers of the spirochete to enter the uninfected person's body. However, it takes only one of the microbacterial spirochetes to transmit the infection, and that spirochete can pass from one body to another in a mere touch.

How do you know you have it?

Usually the first indication that you have syphilis is the appearance of a chancre. This is a painless red sore, often about the size of a pea but occasionally larger or smaller. It usually appears about three to four weeks after contact with an infected person, but it may appear as early as ten days or as late as three months after contact. It occurs at the site where the syphilis bacterium (the spiral-shaped treponema pallidum) invaded the body.

This site will be genital in most cases. In men the chancre appears most often on the glans (or "head") of the penis or in the area just beneath the corona (the ring-like circumference of the glans). It may also appear in the meatus (urinary opening), on the shaft of the penis, or on the scrotum. In women, the chancre will usually appear on the labia majora (external genital lips) or labia minora (interior genital lips), but it may also appear inside the vagina or on the perineum (the area of flesh between the vaginal opening and the anus).

If the chancre does not appear on the genitals, it may develop at other points of sexual contact: the lips of the mouth, the tongue, the inner surfaces of the mouth, the tonsils, the anus, inside the rectum, and, on rare occasions, elsewhere on the body. When a chancre appears on a nonmoist surface, the site usually will be a break in the skin, such as a scratch or bite administered during lovemaking.

In most cases, only one chancre develops, but it is possible for multiple chancres to appear. When they do, the site will usually be parts of the genitals that touch each other: for instance, the underside of the penis and the adjoining area of the scrotum, or adjoining surfaces of the labia majora.

When the chancre first appears, its color is a dull dark red. The chancre is raised, but its surface is smooth, much like that of the skin. As days pass, the surface of the chancre usually ruptures and develops into a dark red open sore, which may in turn develop a yellow or gray crusted scab. In about half of all cases, this sore will be surrounded by a thin pink border. The edges of the chancre often will be raised and hard, like the circumference of a button. This hardness may extend to the base of the chancre and eventually to the surrounding tissue, causing the entire region of flesh to feel hard and rubber-like. In a few cases the chancre will bleed, but generally there will be no bleeding. Whatever its form, the chancre is painless unless secondary bacterial infection develops.

It is possible to have syphilis without observing a chancre. Sometimes the chancre will develop unnoticed in the rectum, throat, or some other interior part of the body. In other cases, there will be no chancre. If you wash with antiseptic soap immediately after sexual contact, the medication in the soap may destroy most of the syphilis bacteria. But don't rely on this to prevent infection. One or more spirochetes may pass through the skin, thus transmitting the disease, even though the concentration of spirochetes in the area is not sufficient to produce a chancre.

The development of a chancre may also be inhibited by antibiotics and other drugs. For instance, you may be taking penicillin, tetracycline, or some other drug for an infected tooth. The dosage may be too low to overcome the infection of syphilis but high enough to prevent a chancre from forming. This same situation may occur several days after you've stopped taking an antibiotic: enough remains in your bloodstream to prevent formation of a chancre but not enough to protect you against the disease.

Occasionally when a chancre develops it will be mistaken for some other form of lesion. It can look like a fever blister or canker sore. When it occurs near the anus it can resemble an anal fissure. Even on the penis it may seem like a different type of growth; Rowan once examined a patient who had a massive growth on the foreskin: Rowan's initial impression was that the patient had cancer of the penis, but testing revealed the growth to be a chancre.

Often the chancre will be accompanied by swelling of nearby lymph nodes. This usually takes place a few days after the chancre appears. The swelling generally is painless, but there may be some tenderness, as in the swollen glands that accompany a sore throat.

If none of these symptoms persuades you to seek treatment, you will be setting yourself up for the second — and far more serious — stage of the disease. Within one to eight weeks, the swelling will subside and the chancre will disappear. Some people will develop a thin, faint scar where the chancre was, but most people will not have any sign whatever of the disease. Unfortunately, the disease remains.

The second stage generally is ushered in with a rash, which

usually develops about six weeks after the appearance of the chancre but may develop as early as two weeks or as late as six months. The rash takes different forms in different people. The only common factor in most cases is that it neither itches nor hurts.

The most common form of syphilitic rash appears as raised bumps of different sizes on the chest, back, arms, legs, face, palms, or soles. The tipoff to diagnosticians is the appearance of the rash on the palms and soles; rashes do not generally affect these areas. On white skin the bumps of the rash first appear cherry- or ham-colored, then turn coppery or brown. On yellow or red skin, the bumps initially are purplish brown and become dark brown or almost black. On black skin, they are grayish blue. When the rash appears on the face, it may form ring-like patterns. On the palms and soles, the bumps generally do not rise above the surface of the skin; the skin may flake off, giving the bumps a shiny appearance.

In warm, moist areas of the body, such as the perineum and the cleft between the buttocks, the rash may take the form of large, flat-topped warts. Called condylomata lata, they are moist and dull red or pink, with a grayish-white surface that eventually ruptures, oozing a clear fluid. The fluid contains large numbers of the syphilis bacteria and is extremely contagious.

The rash may also affect the mucous membrane of the lips, cheeks, tongue, tonsils, and throat. In these areas it also appears in grayish-white patches surrounded by a dull pink or red border. The mucous patches often will be accompanied by hoarseness and a mild sore throat.

In a few people the rash may take a much milder form, appearing only on the shoulders, upper arms, chest, back, and abdomen. The spots will be small, round, and rose-pink. Sometimes they will be quite difficult to see. As with more pronounced rashes, there will be no pain or itching. After several days to several weeks, the spots will turn brownish, rather like the color of freckles, then fade away.

No matter how severe the rash — or even if none appears — about one person in four who has reached the secondary stage of syphilis will have the general discomforts that accompany a bad cold or other infection. These may include frequent headaches, which for unknown reasons usually become worse at night; a low, persistent fever; aching in the long bones, muscles, and joints; loss of appetite, often accompanied by nausea; and swelling of the lymph glands in the neck and armpits. Sometimes the scalp rash will cause the hair to fall in sizable clumps.

While not all symptoms appear in all cases of secondary syphilis, usually there is at least one — most frequently the rash — that is severe enough to prompt the victim to seek medical attention. If treated at this stage, the disease can still be cured before permanent bodily damage is done. But if the disease goes untreated, or if treatment is inadequate, a final and often disabling or even fatal stage begins.

The symptoms of secondary syphilis, like those of the primary form of the disease, vanish whether or not there is treatment. With secondary syphilis, all symptoms generally vanish within two to six weeks. Now the victim is in the stage called latent, or inactive, syphilis.

It is, in most cases, an apparently disease-free state. Three persons in four will have no symptoms whatever. The remaining one in four will have a temporary relapse of primary and secondary symptoms, generally during the first two years of latent syphilis, then return to an asymptomatic state. After about one year of symptom-free latent syphilis, the victim is no longer infectious to other people, except in the case of a pregnant woman who transmits the disease through her bloodstream to her unborn child.

At this point, two people in three are really free of the disease. While they still possess the bacterium treponema pallidum (which will reveal itself in blood tests), they will suffer no further harm or even inconvenience. Apparently the body builds its own defenses against the bacterium.

Of the remaining one in three, about half will suffer no permanent damage. They will develop benign late syphilis, the principal effect of which is a scar, called a gumma, on or in the digestive organs, liver, lungs, eyes, skin, muscles, or endocrine glands. If not treated, the gumma can impede and eventually halt the functioning of the organ; however, the gumma is quickly recognized and easily treated: when it is treated adequately, it usually heals promptly and the patient recovers completely. Benign late syphilis generally appears between three and seven years after the initial infection.

Unfortunately, not all late syphilis is benign. Of the remaining cases, about half will develop neurosyphilis and the other half will develop cardiovascular late syphilis. Neurosyphilis, which develops ten to twenty years after the initial infection, attacks the spinal cord and brain, causing paralysis and loss of mental function. Cardiovascular late syphilis, which develops ten to forty years after the initial infection, attacks the heart and circulatory system, eventually causing death in a small number of victims. Neither of these late forms of syphilis is curable.

In sum, everyone who contracts syphilis begins with PRIMARY SYPHILIS, which is curable. Those who go untreated progress to SECONDARY SYPHILIS, which also is curable. Those who still go untreated enter the stage of LATENT SYPHILIS, from which about 65 percent emerge unscathed; about 17 percent develop BENIGN LATE (or TERTIARY) SYPHILIS, which is curable; about 8 percent develop NEUROSYPHILIS, which usually leads to permanent nerve and brain damage; and about 10 percent develop CARDIOVASCULAR SYPHILIS, which usually leads to permanent damage of the heart and blood vessels.

How is syphilis diagnosed?

Laboratory diagnosis may be made definitively on the basis of finding the spirochete itself or finding certain changes within the blood that inevitably result from the disease.

If a chancre is present, fluid is extracted from it and examined under a dark-field microscope. This microscope employs a light source that projects the beam of light against the side of the delicate and tiny spirochete rather than directly on top of it. Illuminated thus, the difficult-to-see organism seems to glow in the reflected light, and the background appears dark — hence the name, dark-field.

If syphilis is suspected despite absence of a chancre (for

example, in the case of a patient who reports having had a "sore" that "went away"), a spirochete may be found in fluid taken from swollen lymph nodes or, in certain cases, from secondary skin lesions in that area of the body.

Whether or not microscopic examination reveals the treponema pallidum spirochete, syphilis can usually be demonstrated by testing the patient's blood. The original such test was the well-known Wasserman, which since has been supplanted by several others, including the VDRL (developed by Venereal Disease Research Laboratories), the Kahn (named after its discoverer), and the RPCF (Reiter Protein Complement Fixation Test).

The tests do not directly demonstrate the presence of the spirochete. Rather, they reveal the presence in the bloodstream of certain antibodies. An antibody is a chemical produced by the body to fight off harmful organisms. Antibody molecules circulate in the bloodstream and attach themselves to the invading bacteria or other organisms, rendering these organisms more susceptible to destruction by the white blood cells or other elements in the body's chemical self-defense system. Thus, the syphilis blood tests are called "reagin" tests, after the medical term for the appropriate antibodies.

It generally takes four to six weeks for the antibodies to build in the bloodstream. Thus, the initial reagin test may yield a "false negative" result. The test should be repeated one week, one month, and three months later. If all three are negative, it is reasonable to assume that syphilis is not present — provided that there are no other symptoms of syphilis. If other symptoms exist, additional testing should be undertaken, for reagin tests may produce false negatives even after the usual four to six weeks have elapsed.

The tests may also produce false positives, that is, they may suggest syphilis in people who are not infected by the disease. These people generally have some other infection, like mononucleosis, chicken pox, or hepatitis, in defense against which antibodies have been manufactured that closely resemble the antisyphilis antibodies. Early in his medical practice, Robert Rowan encountered such a case. A friend was getting married and wanted Rowan to draw the premarital blood samples. The laboratory to which they were sent reported data indicating that the girl had syphilis. She insisted that she could not because she had never had sexual relations.

A repeat was done on the VDRL, along with several more specific tests. Sure enough, the first test had been a false positive. The girl did not have syphilis. Fortunately, the variety of tests available makes it unnecessary to settle for a false negative or false positive. When diagnosticians have reason to believe a test may be inaccurate, they should challenge the initial results with additional tests. This entails added expense, unfortunately, but it also makes for more accurate diagnosis.

In secondary syphilis, reagin tests prove accurate in a vast majority of cases. Whenever repeat testing fails to erase a diagnostician's doubts, the assumption should be that the patient has syphilis.

Clinical impressions also come into play, depending on patients' activities and circumstances. Take these two cases:

(A) James consults a physician because of a rash on the penis. There are no other symptoms. The rash could, of course, be a symptom of secondary syphilis. But it need not necessarily be.

James has lived for over fifteen years with William. He reports that both had affairs with other men early in their relationship but that in recent years he has not had other partners and he believes William has not had any, either. William has no symptoms. James discussed the rash with him and is confident that William would have told him if there were any possibility he had transmitted it.

An examination reveals no chancre or scar that might indicate an earlier chancre. James's VDRL is negative. Safe conjecture: the rash is not due to syphilis.

(B) Robert has a sore on his anus. It developed four days ago. It is thinner and longer than the typical chancre, but not extremely so.

Robert is a great devotee of sexual variety. In the two weeks before he noticed the sore, he had more than five partners, most of them pickups in bars. Results of dark-field examination: positive for syphilis. Safe assumption: Robert has it.

These cases are, of course, extreme examples that make things very easy for the physician. More often, the clinical picture will be less clear. Thus, a Robert will turn up negative on the VDRL while a James will test positive. The physician's task is to keep testing until the tentative diagnosis is confirmed. A fundamental principle of diagnostic medicine is that one confirms with positive findings, not by exclusion. Thus, a negative on the VDRL would not be reason for concluding that Robert's sore is a result of something other than syphilis. This conclusion would not be warranted even if a dark-field examination of fluids from the sore failed to produce evidence of the spirochete. Testing should continue until all reasonable possibilities, venereal and nonvenereal, have been exhausted.

Once syphilis is diagnosed and treated, follow-up studies should be done at regular intervals. This serves two purposes. First, it ensures that the initial treatment was adequate. Second, it ensures that the person has not been reinfected. The fact is, people who get syphilis once often maintain — and continue to maintain — a life-style that exposes them frequently to reinfection. Actually, if you have more than one sex partner, or if you have only one but your partner has more than one, it's a good idea to have a blood test regularly — say, every three months, or every ten partners, whichever passes first. The blood test is free at most gay health clinics and state and local health department clinics. It can, of course, also be performed by private physicians.

Part of the follow-up testing of someone who has undergone treatment for a confirmed diagnosis of syphilis might be a cerebrospinal fluid (C.S.F.) examination. This is a test of fluid drawn through the spine from the spinal column and brain. It reveals whether the syphilis spirochete has entered the central nervous system. Years ago, the test was routinely administered to people who had been treated for syphilis. It fell into disuse after the development of penicillin, which in normal dosage has proved capable of curing central nervous system (C.N.S.) syphilis. However, recent studies reveal that normal treatment does not always cure C.N.S. syphilis. In one study of a hundred patients with diseases of the central nervous system, thirty-three showed signs of syphilis in the spinal fluid. Seven of these had a history of syphilis; presumably, their treatment proved inadequate. The twenty-six others probably went through the first two stages of syphilis without seeking treatment and perhaps without even realizing that something was wrong.

On the negative side of C.S.F. examinations, the fluid extraction procedure is less than completely safe. Nerve damage can result and occasionally even death when the lumbar puncture (or "spinal tap") is less than perfectly administered. Consequently, health scientists are not unanimous on when to use the procedure.

The position of the Center for Disease Control of the U.S. Public Health Service is that cerebrospinal fluid should be examined in all patients with *suspected* symptomatic neurosyphilis and in other patients with syphilis of greater than a year's duration.

How is it treated?

Treatment for syphilis varies depending on the stage of the disease and whether the victim is pregnant. The drug of choice, universally accepted, is penicillin, with other antibiotics being employed when patients are allergic to penicillin. However, various treatment schedules have been recommended at one time or another by venereologists, with the result that many physicians today prescribe differently for the disease. The treatment schedules most widely accepted for syphilis and other venereal diseases are those formulated by the Venereal Disease Control Advisory Committee of the Public Health Service's Center for Disease Control.

For patients who are allergic to penicillin, the drug of choice is tetracycline. Food and dairy products interfere with absorption; therefore, the pills should be taken at least one hour before and two hours after meals. A second choice for patients allergic to penicillin is erythromycin.

If you have a variety of partners, it is often difficult or impossible to determine who gave the disease to whom. But it is certain that whoever has it will give it to others. If you know where you got it, every one of your partners after that contact is likely to have it. If you don't know where you got it (if, for instance, the symptoms materialize without anyone having warned you that he or she may have infected you), there is a chance that anyone you came into contact with over the past three months has been infected by you.

Public health clinics, on diagnosing syphilis, ask for the names, addresses, and telephone numbers of all the patient's sex partners over a given period, depending on the stage of infection. Clinic employees then contact these people, inform them of their exposure to the disease, and advise them about treatment. Private clinics and physicians in private practice are required under law to report to Public Health Service officials the name of any patient diagnosed as having syphilis. Some physicians and clinics observe the law, others do not. When a patient is reported, health department workers proceed as at public clinics, getting names of partners and contacting them. Physicians and clinics who do not report patients generally expect that the patient will take the responsibility of contacting sex partners and advising them they may be infected.

Whatever position you take on what the law should be and whether physicians should observe it, the fact remains that you may have infected a great many people. If they go unwarned, they may transmit the disease to many others. Those who do not recognize the symptoms and seek help may eventually be severely disabled or even killed by the disease.

How can you avoid syphilis?

The only foolproof way to avoid syphilis is to avoid sex with anyone who might have it — in other words, limit yourself to one partner and make sure that both of you are not infected when your relationship begins. The latter generally will be impractical, to say nothing of impolitic and unaesthetic. However, sex under any other circumstance does involve the risk of syphilis, and the risk increases in direct proportion to your number of partners and their number of partners.

Limiting yourself to one or another mode of sexual congress will not reduce the risk. Syphilis can be transmitted by the mouth and anus as well as the genitals, and can even be transmitted through nonsexual touching. Chances of transmission increase considerably if contact is made with a chancre or condyloma containing rich stores of the treponema pallidum spirochete. However, syphilis is also transmitted by asymptomatic carriers. Genital contact is probably the principal mode: penis to vagina, penis to mouth, penis to anus, vulva to mouth, or any of these in reverse. However, nongenital transmission is far from infrequent; the modes include anus to mouth and mouth to mouth.

Can simple kissing transmit syphilis? Indeed. Rowan is familiar with a case of two women who shared an apartment. One developed a sore on her lip. The other, a nurse, suggested that she get a blood test because she might have syphilis. The first woman said she was positive she was not infected; she might sleep around occasionally, but she certainly wasn't promiscuous — and she always kept herself "clean." Before the nurse could reply, her roommate added, "I'll prove that it's not syphilis!" Whereupon she kissed the nurse on the lips. A week later the nurse developed a sore on her lip. She had syphilis.

Theoretically syphilis can be transmitted by a contaminated towel or drinking cup or any other interpersonally exchanged item. Actually, these methods of transmission are too rare to merit serious consideration. The spirochete is so sensitive that it cannot survive for more than a few seconds outside the human body.

Will it help to inspect a partner's body for sores before having sex? It can. If your prospective partner has an open sore, especially in the area of the genitals, anus, or mouth, it's a good idea at least to inquire about a recent examination for syphilis. Remember that many people do not know what the disease is, and others do not know that it is contagious.

A condom will offer men partial protection against syphilis. If the chancre is inside a partner's vagina, rectum, or mouth, the condom can prevent spirochetes that may be harbored there from making direct contact with the penis. However, such protection is far from complete: the spirochetes can be transmitted from the condom to a moist surface of the skin after penile withdrawal, or they can travel along the moist outer surface of the condom and enter the body through the flesh of the abdomen, scrotum, or thighs.

CHAPTER 3

Gonorrhea

(Transmitted Homosexually Almost Exclusively among Men)

What is it?

It is a bacterial infection, usually of the urinary tract but also found in other moist areas of the body, including the throat, rectum, and eyes. In the vernacular, it's known as "the clap." The infectious bacterium is the gonococcus.

How do you get it?

Like the treponema pallidum bacterium, which carries syphilis, the gonococcus is extremely fragile. Thus, it is not transmitted through the air (as may be the streptococcus) or on utensils or clothing (as may be the pneumococcus). Barring a few cases that are so rare that they barely merit mention, gonorrhea is transmitted only by sexual contact.

Moreover, in most cases there must be fairly prolonged contact of moist bodily surfaces. Unlike the spiral-shaped treponema pallidum, which can burrow its way into a victim almost in the instant that contact is made, the gonococcus needs virtually to be implanted in a moist area. The penis may implant it in the vagina, rectum, or throat. The penile urethra may attract it from the vagina or rectum and perhaps from the throat, though there is no conclusive evidence that this latter mode of transmission is possible. The bacterium may be implanted in the eye, a particularly hospitable environment, by even the most casual contact — if, for example, the eye is rubbed by a finger that has just touched a gonorrheal discharge. But other modes of transmission are virtually unheard of. This, no doubt, is why gonorrhea is a serious problem among heterosexually active people and homosexually active men but not among women whose activity is exclusively homosexual.

Actually, even if one partner is known to be infected, it is not certain that the other(s) will contract the disease. The bacteria do not always obtain a foothold in the uninfected person. They often die in the transfer. Studies suggest that penile intromission (vaginally or anally) with a person known to be infected will result in transmission of the disease less than half the time.

But there is small consolation in this statistic. The more contacts there are — the more any sex act is repeated with the infected person — the greater the likelihood of contagion. In the United States and Canada today, there are more carriers of gonorrhea — some symptomatic, others asymptomatic — than of all other major venereal diseases combined. Indeed, two and a half million North Americans are believed to have the disease at any given time. That means one person in a hundred is infected. More than half of the infectees are under twenty-five. More than half live in urban areas. In some cities, as much as 20 percent of the population aged fifteen to twenty-five may have gonorrhea.

Gonorrhea is not nearly as dangerous in terms of mortality or the potential for permanent disability. The disease-carrying bacterium is not nearly so hearty. Yet, the sheer preponderance of cases makes this millennia-old malady an extremely serious health problem.

Millennia-old? The Greek physician Hippocrates described gonorrhea in 400 B.C. He believed it resulted from "excessive indulgence in the pleasures of Venus." Modern physicians know that it's not a question of how often but with whom. Nonetheless, considering that frequency of contact with an infectious source enhances the prospects of contagion, one can respect that Hippocrates's theory had empirical basis.

For a number of years after the discovery of penicillin, it was mistakenly believed that a gonorrheal infection was of no major consequence. A simple shot of penicillin, people were fond of saying, quickly cures the disease. Thus — so the story went — "the clap" is no more serious than catching a cold. Occasionally one still sees this statement in newspapers and magazines.

Don't believe it. Gonorrhea is capable of producing multiple complications that you never get with the common cold. It is resistant to many antibiotics and can survive within the body even after therapy. If not successfully treated, it can cause long-term and occasionally permanent damage.

At its onset, gonorrhea is a surface infection of the walls of the body cavity that it infects — the urethra, vagina, mouth, rectum. However, it may spread by the blood stream to other areas of the body, or it can progress along the surface of the infected cavity to adjacent areas.

From the male urethra — the most common site of infection — the gonococci may move into the prostate gland, where they can produce serious inflammation with generalized symptoms, such as chills and fever. The infection can also pass down the vas deferens — that is, the duct that connects the urethra to the testicle — and infect the epididymis, the organ at the juncture of the vas and the testicle. In these cases, an inflammation and infection called "epididymitis" develops. The scrotum becomes swollen, painful, tender, and hot. The pain is severe, and even the slightest movement aggravates it. Chills and fever accompany the infection, and when both testicles are involved, sterility can result.

In women, gonococci move upward from the vagina through the cervix into the uterus, then into the fallopian tubes. They nest there, creating abcesses that produce all the symptoms of general abdominal infection: pain, swelling, chills, fever. Sometimes there is also blood on urination. If the woman is not treated promptly, the tube may be permanently blocked. Since these tubes transport egg cells from the ovaries to the uterus for fertilization, blockage of one tube reduces by half the woman's ability to conceive. If both tubes are blocked, the woman becomes sterile.

When gonococcus bacteria enter the bloodstream, they can be carried to just about any point in the body, including the joints, the heart valves, and even the corpus callosum, or brain covering. If treatment is not prompt and efficacious, the result can be permanent disability or death — although this rarely happens, because the seriousness of the symptoms usually prompts victims to seek medical attention.

The eyes are particularly vulnerable to gonococci. Infection rarely reaches this site systemically, but bacteria can be transmitted by touch or even spray. If this latter possibility seems remote, bear in mind that even barely visible droplets of the gonorrheal discharge can carry more than enough bacteria to transmit infection.

Not surprisingly, if the bacterium can infect the eyes easily, it can infect other moist bodily surfaces. During fellatio, an infected penis almost certainly will discharge pus into the mouth. During anal intercourse pus will be discharged into the rectum. This can happen, of course, even if ejaculation does not take place. The pus of gonorrhea is perfectly capable of evacuating the urethra without prostatic propulsion.

Among homosexually active women, gonorrhea is not such a problem. The female anatomy does not encourage its spread from woman to woman. If the vagina discharges pus, this usually is noticed and sexual activity is suspended until the condition is treated.

In 90 percent of all cases, female gonorrhea is asymptomatic in the early stages. This does not prevent the disease from spreading to men, whose penes plumb the depths of the vagina where the organism is housed; however, apparently there is little if any spread through cunnilingus. Quite possibly gonorrhea might be transmitted between women if a vibrator is promptly transferred from the vagina of someone who is infected to that of someone who is not.

How do you know you have it?

Often you don't. As has been noted, a carrier state exists in up to 90 percent of all early-stage female victims and up to 10 percent of all early-stage male victims. If you are a carrier, the only ways you learn that you have the disease are if (a) someone who catches it from you tells you, or (b) the disease progresses to a later stage, which produces more serious symptoms.

Once gonorrhea bacteria enter a hospitable bodily cavity

(urethra, vagina, rectum, throat), the body's defensive system responds by sending white blood cells through the bloodstream to the infected area. These white blood cells attack and consume some of the bacteria, and the resultant matter is pus. The discharge of this pus from the infected cavity is the first symptom of the disease.

However, a discharge in the throat is evacuated through the esophagus into the stomach; thus, until other symptoms appear — inflammation, swelling — the infection goes undetected. Likewise, a discharge from the rectum may go unnoticed unless it is so profuse that it issues through the anus at times other than during defecation.

The incubation time — that is, the time between exposure to infection and onset of symptoms — usually is three to five days, but it may be less than a day or as long as a month. A few cases from Rowan's files illustrate the extremes.

• Thomas phoned from the airport. His penile drip had just started. Six hours before his flight, he had had sexual relations for the first time in almost a year.

• Leonard had relations at 8 P.M. His penile discharge started the next morning.

• Ted had sex on New Year's Eve. He remembers the date well, because he met his partner at a party and had no subsequent sexual contact for four weeks. The penile discharge appeared on February 1, and the diagnosis of gonorrhea was confirmed with laboratory tests.

What exactly does the penile discharge look like? It resembles the pus that may develop at the site of any bodily infection. It is usually white, but it may be yellow or yellowish-green. It may be thin, clear, and mucus-like, or it may be heavy, thick, and creamy.

Other symptoms of gonorrhea when the site is the penis:

• The lips of the meatus (the urethral opening at the head of the penis) become swollen and stand out from the glans.

• There is pain or burning at the meatus or throughout the urethra during urination; the pain may be quite intense, and urination may be difficult.

• Urine is clouded with pus and may contain blood.

• In uncircumcised men, there may be redness and irritation of the glans and the area of the shaft under the foreskin.

Vaginal gonorrhea, as has been noted, will in 90 percent of all cases fail to produce symptoms. In the remaining cases, there will be a discharge. It may be thick, heavy, and creamy, or thin, clear, and mucus-like. As is true with men, if you have a discharge, you have a problem; get medical attention.

Gonorrheal infection of the anus and rectum, called gonococcal proctitis, usually is asymptomatic. When symptoms appear, they usually take the form of mild irritation and/or a mucous discharge. In some cases there will be pain on defecation and/or blood or pus in the feces.

Oral gonorrhea is essentially an infection of the throat. Technically, it is a pharyngitis, but more specifically a gonorrheal pharyngitis, as opposed to streptococcal (another bacterium) pharyngitis or some other sort of infection.

The throat is the only portion of the oral cavity that has the proper climate for the disease to establish itself. Thus, unlike syphilis, gonorrhea cannot infect the tongue, lips, inner cheeks, or gums.

The primary symptom is usually soreness, as in the classic "sore throat," about three to five days after sexual contact. There is redness of the tonsils and walls of the throat, and there may be a pus-like discharge. There usually will also be fever and swelling of the lymph glands on the side of the neck.

Note: These symptoms are the same as those of your everyday garden-variety sore throat, but if a physician treats you for the latter, the medication usually will not be strong enough to kill the gonococcal bacteria. Therefore, do not simply describe the symptoms; *tell* the physician that you've performed fellatio and suspect you may have been infected that way.

Not surprisingly, victims of gonorrhea frequently do not want their wives or other steady partners to know they have had extracurricular relations. This may result in their trying to get the unknowing partner to seek medical aid without knowing the real reason.

Some of the proposals patients have brought to Rowan in this regard have been:

• Write my wife a letter saying the company I work for wants all the wives checked for long-standing V.D., then treat her as if for an infection of many years' duration.

• Call my wife and tell her I have prostate trouble and she has to be treated to avoid spreading the infection to our children.

• Call my wife's physician and tell him about the problem and have him treat her without her knowing what for.

It is, of course, unfortunate that people feel the need to hide evidence of activity that causes illness. We'll stifle the impulse to dissertate on this subject, other than to say that in recent years, fortunately, the need with respect to sexual activity — whether heterosexual or homosexual — has diminished considerably.

How is gonorrhea diagnosed?

A "smear" — or specimen — of the discharge is taken on a glass slide. When the site of infection is the urethra, the discharge is transferred directly to the slide. With other sites, the discharge is collected on a cotton swab and transferred. Whatever the mode of collection, the material from the discharge is allowed to dry, then is stained with a dye that differentiates the various strains of bacteria, and is viewed through a microscope. Gonorrhea has a characteristic red color, is found in pairs, and is located within the white cells of the discharge. In technical language, this set of circumstances is described as "gram negative, intracellular diplococci."

There are times when a smear will not be sufficient to make a diagnosis. Then a more advanced study, called a "culture," is required. The specimen is multiplied by incubation on a "growth medium" (that is, a quantity of vegetable matter at optimal temperature and climate for the bacterium's development). The multiplication of bacteria produces groups called colonies, which have a characteristic appearance, on the basis of which identification is made.

If a urethral smear cannot be obtained by simple "milking" of the penis, an additional discharge usually can be produced by prostatic massage. That is, the diagnostician places a finger in the rectum and gently massages the prostate gland. This pressure should cause the gland to expel secretions that pass through the urethra. A smear and culture can be made of this material, and if gonococci are present, they will usually be found.

What happens if gonorrhea goes untreated? That depends on the site of the infection.

If gonococcal urethritis (that is, gonococcal infection of the urethra) is not treated within a few days after symptoms appear, the infection spreads up the urethra. Pain on urination becomes more severe, and bacteria invade the glands that lubricate the urethra. In some cases, they also invade the deeper tissues of the penis.

And then? After about two weeks, the symptoms begin to disappear. The discharge is lighter, and urination is no longer as painful. However, as with syphilis, the bacteria are still present, and partners can be infected.

After two to three weeks of untreated infection, the bacteria reach the deeper portions of the urethra and the prostate gland. In 5 to 10 percent of untreated men, an abscess will form within the prostate gland, causing a sensation of heat, along with pain or swelling, in the lower pelvis or around the anus. This generally will be accompanied by a high fever and severe pain on defecation. Also, the enlarged, infected prostate presses on the bladder and/or urethra, making urination difficult or impossible.

In another 20 percent of untreated men, the infection will spread down the vasa deferentia, the tubes through which sperm cells travel on their way from the testicles to the prostate gland for discharge in the semen at the time of ejaculation. At the base of each vas deferens is a small organ called an epididymis. The infection lodges in one or both epididymides, causing pain in the groin, a sensation of heaviness in the infected testicle, and the formation of a small, hard, painful swelling at the base of the infected testicle. The overlying skin of the scrotum reddens, feels hot, and is painful.

Even when treated, gonococcal epididymitis, as the infection is called, leaves scar tissue which may block the vas deferens. If both epididymides are infected — which may happen when the infection of a single epididymis goes untreated — the man may become sterile.

In the female, untreated vaginal gonorrhea may enter the uterus and fallopian tubes, producing abdominal pain, swelling, fever, chills, and sometimes blood on urination. If this infection is not treated promptly, there may be permanent blockage of one or both tubes, diminishing fertility in the former instance, causing sterility in the latter.

A majority of women, however, will not experience these complications, just as most men will not suffer gonococcal epididymitis — even though their gonorrhea goes untreated. They will lose their original symptoms and feel just fine. But they may be carriers of the disease, infecting partner after partner after partner without suspecting that anything is wrong until one of these partners traces the infection to its source.

There is no easily seen site of advanced infection for sufferers of anorectal gonorrhea (medical term: gonorrheal proctitis) or oral gonorrhea (gonorrheal pharyngitis). If the disease is not treated, symptoms will eventually disappear and the person will be an asymptomatic carrier.

However, in about one percent of all cases of untreated gonorrhea, the gonococci will break away from the infected cavity and enter the bloodstream. This happens somewhat more often with oral and anorectal gonorrhea than with the genital variety, but we stress that it can happen no matter what the original site of the infection.

When any kind of bacterium infects the bloodstream, the condition is termed septicemia. If not treated promptly, gonococcal septicemia can lead to permanent damage of the heart, liver, central nervous system, and joints. By far the most common complication is damage of the joints — especially the knees, wrists, knuckles, ankles, and elbows, in that order. Heart, liver, and central nervous system damage is rare. The main symptoms of gonococcal septicemia are fever, chills, loss of appetite, and pain in one or more joints.

How is it treated?

As with syphilis, the treatment for gonorrhea will depend on the stage of the disease and whether the victim is pregnant. The drug of choice, universally accepted, is penicillin, with other antibiotics being employed when patients are allergic to penicillin.

Unsymptomatic persons who are known to have been exposed to gonorrhea should receive the same treatment as those whose infection is proven. All patients with gonorrhea should have their blood tested for syphilis at the time that gonorrhea is diagnosed. If the test is negative, there is no need for follow-up tests if the patient is being treated for gonorrhea with the preferred penicillin schedule. However, patients treated with ampicillin, tetracycline, or spectinomycin should have a follow-up test after three months to detect inadequately treated syphilis.

Patients who have gonorrhea and also syphilis should be treated for both concurrently. Although long-acting forms of penicillin, such as benzathine penicillin G, are effective for treatment of syphilis, they do not cure gonorrhea. Therefore, a separate gonorrhea regimen must be administered.

If you have difficulty urinating, whether or not you have been treated for gonorrhea, it's a good idea to get immediate medical attention. If impairment is not due to a urethral stricture, it may be the result of prostate enlargement or some other condition that can prove fatal if it goes untreated.

Often after adequate treatment of gonorrhea, a penile drip will remain. It may be caused by infection, irritation, or other phenomena.

At times, gonorrhea is accompanied by a secondary bacterial infection. The bacterium chlamydia trachomatis is not affected by penicillin. Thus, gonorrhea is cured and the secondary infection remains. It is not dangerous, but it may be bothersome — and infectious.

At other times, gonorrhea is accompanied by a secondary viral infection. This poses a difficult problem, because at present there are no simple tests to demonstrate the presence of viruses. Moreover, there is no adequate treatment. You can only hope the condition goes away.

In still other situations, though there will be no secondary infection, an anxious patient may produce irritation by frequently "milking" the penis to see if the discharge has yet vanished. Repeated "milking" can cause the multiple glands that line the urethra to start secreting protective fluids. These fluids are the products of irritation, not infection, but they may be mistaken for infection.

When a person contracts gonorrhea, especially for the first time, he or she may decide to forego sexual activity completely for a period of time. In men, the prostate gland will continue to manufacture the materials that compose semen. These materials and others from accessory organs empty into the urethra and produce what appears to be an infectious discharge. Actually, it is a normal physiologic response.

The prostate, meanwhile, may become congested with materials that are not emptied into the urethra. The congestion generally continues until the patient resumes having sex.

Congestive prostatitis is a result of deviation from sexual routine. A great deal more sex than usual or a great deal less can bring on the condition. The congestion may be accompanied by inflammation and a persistent urethral discharge. The condition may subside on its own or may require treatment with antibiotics.

How do you avoid gonorrhea?

Short of not having sexual relations, the best way to prevent gonorrhea is to wear a condom. Unlike syphilis, whose bacteria may work their way around a condom, the gonococcus appears unable to survive unless implanted directly in mucous membrane. A condom will protect the wearer from contracting penile gonorrhea from the vagina, anus, throat (if throat-to-penis transmission is possible), or penis (there is a case on record of gonorrhea being transmitted from penis to penis during simple hugging — apparently one partner's urethral meatus came into contact with the other partner's discharge). If the wearer of the condom is infected, his partner(s) will be protected against contracting the disease from his penis — though, of course, he may also have anal infection which could be transmitted to someone not wearing a condom.

Many men do not like to wear condoms. If you don't wear one, you may get slight protection against gonorrhea by urinating and washing your penis immediately after sex. Neither of these measures is very reliable, but they're better than nothing.

CHAPTER 4

Nonspecific Urethritis (N.S.U.)

(Transmitted Homosexually Exclusively among Men)

What is it?

It is a nongonococcal infection of the urethra. The term "nonspecific" is somewhat misleading. Actually, several infectious bacteria or viruses have been identified, and it is possible to prove that a particular infection is indeed the result of one of these *specific* agents. However, the symptoms, diagnosis, and treatment are identical, whatever the agent. Consequently, venereologists classify the entire group as N.S.U.

How do you get it?

It certainly is transmitted sexually, but cases occasionally develop in monogamous couples and even in people who do not have any sexual activity whatever. Venereologist H. Hunter Handsfield, of the University of California at Irvine, has surveyed reported cases and calculates that somewhat less than 85 percent were definitely transmitted sexually. Up to 10 percent appear to have been transmitted nonsexually, and the remainder may or may not have been transmitted sexually.

Among sexually transmitted cases that he surveyed, about 40 percent involved the bacterium chlamydia trachomatis; fewer than 5 percent were related to the organism trichomonas vaginalis; rare cases appeared to be related to herpesvirus hominis, to intraurethral venereal warts (more about this in Chapter 15), and to syphilis (intraurethral chancre); the balance involved unknown organisms.

Among cases transmitted nonsexually, Dr. Handsfield found that infection might be secondary to urethral stricture, to phimosis (narrowness of the opening of the prepuce, preventing its being drawn back over the glans), or to catheterization or other instrumental invasion of the urethra. Infection might also be associated with urinary tract infections, including bacterial prostatitis, or related to urethral stricture, allergic conditions, or trauma (specifically, "milking" the penis).

Sexual transmission must, logically enough, involve the penis. When transmission is homosexual, it generally is the result of anorectal contact. Neither of us has ever heard of N.S.U. having been transmitted orally or manually, nor has any venereologist with whom we have discussed the subject. When transmission is heterosexual, it may be by vaginal or anorectal contact.

Anorectally transmitted N.S.U. appears to be more severe than that transmitted vaginally. This is true whether one's partner happens to be male or female. Probably the reason for greater severity anorectally is that there are both a greater concentration and a wider variety of bacteria, viruses, fungi, and other infectious agents in the intestinal tract.

When you consider that there is a much higher incidence of anorectal intromission homosexually than heterosexually, it is not surprising that urethritis among homosexually active men is more severe, persistent, recurrent, and difficult to treat than among men whose activity is exclusively heterosexual.

How do you know you have it?

An inflammation of the urethra develops within a month of sexual contact. The first symptoms usually appear after three days, but they may appear sooner. The chief symptoms are a watery discharge from the urethra, burning on urination, and at times urinary frequency. The discharge may be continuous, but in many cases it is present only in the morning, before urination. In some cases, no actual discharge appears unbidden, but the fluid can be produced by "milking" the penis. Whatever its frequency, the discharge usually is thin, clear, and whitish, as opposed to the discharge from gonorrhea, which typically is thick, white-to-yellow, and creamy. However, there are exceptions in N.S.U. where the discharge is visually indistinguishable from that of gonorrhea: the only way they can be told apart is by laboratory testing.

The more common infectious agents in N.S.U. are:

• The bacterium chlamydia trachomatis, also known familiarly as "trick." The vernacular term, also used for trichomonas vaginalis, derives from "TRIC-agent," used to describe two rather indistinguishable infectious agents, one of which causes trachoma and the other inclusion conjunctivitis.

• Mycoplasmata. A mycoplasm is a microscopic organism similar in character to bacteria but closer in size to a virus (which is much smaller than a bacterium). There are several mycoplasmata that have been identified in the discharge of N.S.U., most of them of the T-strain variety.

• Intestinal bacteria, such as the escherichia coli, principal bacterium in feces, and hemophilus.

• Local allergy. That is, the urethra and meatus are irritated by dyes in clothing or by soaps, chemical sprays, or other foreign agents.

Some diagnosticians differentiate between N.S.U. and nongonococcal urethral infections of known cause — for instance, allergic chemical reactions, infection from intestinal bacteria, or traumatic urethritis caused by "milking" the penis. Again, however, for all practical purposes, these are classifiable as N.S.U.

How is N.S.U. diagnosed? _____

With N.S.U., positive findings may point definitively to one or more of the infectious agents listed earlier. If not, other likely causes of the symptoms are ruled out: gonorrhea, tuberculosis, or cancer of the urethra. When all other known causes of the symptoms have been eliminated, the "diagnosis" is N.S.U.

Just how far to go in testing for other causes is a matter of judgment. For example, among the tests one might perform in search of urethral cancer or other disease are an intravenous pyelogram, which involves filling the urinary tract with a dye, then x-raying it; cystoscopy, or insertion of a viewing instrument into the urethra and bladder; and panendoscopy, or cystoscopy with a more sophisticated instrument that permits visualization of the entire interior of the bladder. One might also perform urine studies for tuberculosis and other diseases.

Most of these tests are expensive, and some of them have danger of serious side effects. In intravenous pyelography, for example, there is a danger of allergic reaction, which can be permanently damaging or even fatal. In cystoscopy and panendoscopy, there is danger of infection, bleeding, and even death from the use of anesthesia. There is no point in subjecting the patient to these risks and burdens if there is not a *good chance* that his problem is something more than simple N.S.U.

It has been established that N.S.U. occurs with particular frequency among people who recently were infected with gonorrhea. This may be because the other organisms invaded the urethra at the same time as the gonococcus but were masked by it; when gonorrhea is cured, the nongonococcal infection remains.

How is N.S.U. treated?

Some cases require no treatment. Within a week or two of their initial appearance, the symptoms disappear, and there is no further problem. Quite probably this fortuitous development is the result of the infectious organisms being washed from the urethra during urination. A heartier organism, like the gonococcus, would take hold much too firmly to be washed away.

If the infection does not go away on its own, it will usually respond to antibiotics. The Center for Disease Control (C.D.C.) Advisory Committee has not issued recommendations, but there is a consensus among venereologists for tetracycline as the agent of first choice and doxycycline or minocycline as second choices. A third choice, mainly used when patients are allergic to the other drugs, is erythromycin.

Many physicians, Rowan among them, believe that coffee, alcoholic beverages, and spices should be avoided during treatment because they exacerbate the infection and possibly interfere with the results of treatment. Other physicians argue that there is no evidence that these substances create any problems. While controlled studies have not been done, it is Rowan's clinical impression that treatment progresses better among patients who avoid the substances.

In some cases, N.S.U. that has been successfully treated appears to have been reactivated as long as a year after treatment by consumption of large quantities of alcohol — say, the equivalent of five or six ounces of pure alcohol over twenty-four hours. Again, there is no definitive evidence, but clinical impressions point in this direction. Alumni of N.S.U. may therefore wish to avoid alcohol in these volumes — or if they do not, they will at least have a theory about how the recurrence developed.

Treatment with antibiotics is effective about 80 percent of the time. When it is ineffective, more extensive diagnostic procedures should be employed. If none of these procedures produces definitive results, the patient may well be one of that fortunately relatively small group that contracts N.S.U. for life.

How can you avoid N.S.U.?

Not knowing what causes the disease(s), we can only speculate about how to avoid it (them). A condom will prevent the spread of some and possibly all bacteria, just as it prevents the spread of gonorrhea. Washing the penis and urinating immediately after sex may also help. Fortunately, the complications of N.S.U. are relatively inconsequential; thus prevention is not as serious a matter as with syphilis, gonorrhea, and other more damaging infections.

A final note regarding chlamydia trachomatis organisms: Trachoma is a serious and possibly permanently damaging eye infection, principally among adults. It is not normally thought of as genitally related, though there is no evidence that it is *not* genitally related. It sometimes is known as "swimming pool conjunctivitis," because it frequently is contracted in pools that have not been chlorinated. Genital infection in adults may cause eye infection in babies similar to the infection caused by gonorrhea but usually less destructive.

CHAPTER 5

Nonspecific Vaginitis (N.S.V.)

(Transmitted Homosexually Exclusively among Women)

What is it?

It is the female version of gonorrhea without the gonococcus. As with urethritis in the male, there are several types of vaginal infections. The two most common, trichomonas and monilia, also appear in the male. The remaining infections generally are referred to as nonspecific vaginitis, even though the infectious agent may be known, as in the case of the bacterium hemophilus vaginalis, also called corynebacterium vaginale. This lumping together of disease entities is not so much a matter of nosological laziness or antifeminism (men, after all, have *their* diseases classified) as it is a reflection of the fact that all of the infections are quite mild, have the same symptoms, and are easily treated. Indeed, there is some dispute among scientists whether hemophilus vaginalis and the other N.S.V. conditions are even diseases. It may just be that the organisms in question are benign (as opposed to infectious) and just happen to have been found in the vaginas of women who reported N.S.V. symptoms. The same organisms have been found in women who did not have symptoms. Whether they occur more frequently in symptomatic women has not, to our knowledge, been investigated. This absence of investigation is not so much a matter of indifference on the part of medical science as a reflection, again, of the relative harmlessness and easy treatment of N.S.V.

None of which is to say that N.S.V. is an imaginary entity. Its symptoms, as any woman knows who has suffered them, are very real. The main symptom is a vaginal discharge. This usually is thin and colorless or slightly cloudy, but it occasionally may be thick and whitish, like the discharge of gonorrhea. The discharge generally is accompanied by an itchy sensation inside the vagina. Very rarely the woman will also have chills and a fever.

How do you get it?

N.S.V. has been known to develop in women who have no sex relations whatever and in others who are involved in a monogamous relationship. Thus, it is not always transmitted sexually. It appears more frequently among women who are not monogamous, but the extent to which this datum demonstrates sexual transmission remains open to question. There is no evidence at present of more or less N.S.V. among women whose activity is exclusively homosexual, exclusively heterosexual, or ambisexual.

There is no question, however, that N.S.V. is communicable both heterosexually and homosexually.

The organisms can be carried from one vagina to the other on the fingers and hands or on a vibrator or dildo. It is questionable whether cunnilingus can also transmit N.S.V., but in most cases the question is academic, since the same mouth would have to have contact with both vaginas. If sex play includes anorectal contact, infectious organisms of the intestinal tract might be brought to the vagina on the fingers or a mechanical device and possibly by mouth.

N.S.V., however, may be transmitted nonsexually. Thus, the fact that one develops the condition does not mean that a partner transmitted it. On the other hand, the person who has it may very well give it to someone else. Therefore, during the treatment period it is wise to avoid the kinds of contact that can transfer the organisms to a partner.

How is N.S.V. diagnosed?

The hemophilus vaginalis bacterium reveals itself readily when viewed under a microscope. Other specific organisms of

N.S.V. are identifiable also, but few physicians bother to try identifying them because identification has no bearing on treatment.

The usual procedure when a patient has a vaginal discharge is to take a smear of the material and examine it microscopically, using immunofluorescent techniques, and in a culture for gonorrhea. If there are no gonococcus organisms and no history of heterosexual activity, it is reasonable to assume that the infection is nongonococcal.

How is it treated?

If there are pus cells in the discharge, penicillin or other antibiotics may be prescribed. If there are no pus cells, topical treatments will usually bring the condition under control. Many cases of N.S.V., perhaps most cases, can be successfully brought under control with simple home remedies. When symptoms appear, douche once with a solution of water and vinegar (one teaspoon vinegar in one quart of water). If a mild fever and chills develop along with vaginal discharge and itching, the treatment is as for a common cold: drink plenty of water, keep warm, and get ample bed rest.

If the condition does not abate within a week, consult a physician. If the diagnosis is nongonococcal infection (hemophilus vaginalis or other organisms), the treatment of choice is ampicillin. For women who are allergic to penicillin, a first alternate choice is erythromycin; a second choice is azogantanol.

How can you avoid N.S.V.?

Not knowing what causes the disease(s) or even that we are dealing with disease(s), we obviously cannot offer a foolproof formula for avoiding it (them). However, here are some ways to minimize risks:

• Do not use perfumed douches. Chemicals in these preparations may destroy natural vaginal substances that prevent development of N.S.V. Many physicians advise not douching even with plain water except as treatment for specific conditions.

• Wear cotton panties or none at all rather than those made of nylon or other synthetic fibers. The latter do not ventilate as well and create an atmosphere of warmth and moisture more hospitable to the development of N.S.V. organisms.

• Wash your hands before inserting a finger into your own vagina after it has been in a partner's vagina. If anorectal contact takes place, wash your hands (or other organ or instrument) before making contact with the vagina.

• In heterosexual activity, transfer of infectious organisms can be prevented if the man wears a condom. However, many women — and men — find condoms unpleasant and prefer to take their chances with N.S.V.

CHAPTER 6

Trichomoniasis
(Transmitted Homosexually among Men and Women)

What is it?

It is a disease caused by a parasite, the trichomonas vaginalis, a one-celled animal. The parasite got the last part of its name at a time when it was believed to inhabit only the vagina, not the male urethra. Researchers since have discovered that it can exist in men or women. It is sexually transmitted, but it may also be transmitted nonsexually.

As venereal maladies go, trichomoniasis is more an inconvenience than a serious disorder. In women it causes vaginal inflammation and discharge, usually accompanied by itching. In men it causes urethral inflammation and discharge, often accompanied by irritation of the prostate gland.

In women the discharge can be meager or copious; it usually will be frothy, greenish-yellow, and odorous. Generally it is accompanied by a burning sensation in the vagina and the labia.

Men generally will have only a slight discharge, usually with thin, milky liquid, and a mild itching inside the penis. Frequently men and women will be asymptomatic.

How do you get it?

Like all parasitic infestations, trichomoniasis involves the transfer of the parasite from one body to another. This particular parasite is rather hearty and can survive outside the human body for minutes or even hours. Thus, while transmission is very often sexual — probably usually sexual — the infestation may also be transmitted on shared washcloths, towels, clothing, bedsheets, and other objects.

The chief mode of transmission is coitus. When there is sexual transmission between two women, it will be by some means that involves transfer from one vagina to another. This presumably is possible on the fingers, hands, or mouth, or on a mechanical device. However, very rarely is trichomoniasis reported by women whose activity is exclusively homosexual. Thus, we conclude that very little sexual transmission takes place among women.

In men, the trichomoniasis situation is somewhat confused. Homosexual transmission of the parasite trichomonas vaginalis presumably is next to impossible; the animal survives long-term only in the urinary environment, and transfer thus would entail some activity that brought the discharge from urethra to urethra. However, if the organism can stay alive for an hour on a washcloth, it presumably can stay alive at least as long in the rectum. Thus, rectal and possibly oral transmission probably take place at least occasionally.

The situation is further complicated by the existence of two other parasites of the same family: trichomonas hominis, which resides in the intestinal tract (of the female as well as the male, despite the name) and trichomonas buccalis, which resides in the mouth. These organisms, like their vaginalis cousin, can live outside the body for a while. Thus, it is entirely feasible that any of the organisms — genital, rectal, or oral — might be transmitted in any sex act — genital, rectal, or oral — with a partner of either gender.

Note that there are a lot of "probably's" and "presumably's" in the past few paragraphs. Why isn't more definite information available? As with nonspecific vaginitis, medical scientists simply have not investigated the organisms thoroughly because the infestation is quite mild and easily treatable. As one urologist has noted, "I have not seen trichomonas organisms in homosexually active men because I have not looked for them. If I looked for them, I believe I would find them. But there are too many important things to look for; it is a waste of the patient's money to go looking for trichomonas organisms."

A final note on the transmission of trichomoniasis: Once the organisms find their abode, they may lie dormant for weeks or months before producing symptoms. Thus, if you develop symptoms today, it does not necessarily mean that you contracted the organism from your most recent partner; nor does it mean that you transmitted the organism to that partner after catching it from her or his predecessor. You may have contracted the organism long ago, sexually or nonsexually, and you may or may not have transmitted it sexually or nonsexually to some or all of your partners.

How is it diagnosed?

Diagnosis of trichomoniasis is made by examining the discharge under a microscope to observe the parasite. Since the animal is very small, it may be necessary to grow a colony on a culture medium specially prepared for this purpose.

How is it treated?

In women, trichomoniasis can occasionally be overcome without medication. When symptoms appear, douche once with a solution of one teaspoon vinegar in one quart of water. If this treatment is successful, symptoms should abate within two days.

If douching does not evacuate the organisms, the first choice of treatment is metronidazole. If this treatment proves ineffective, or if the woman has an allergic reaction to metronidazole (such reactions are rare), the alternate treatment is to douch with Vagisec solution.

In men, the only recommended treatment is metronidazole. If the infestation persists, the treatment should be repeated four weeks later.

Heterosexual partners and male homosexual partners should be treated simultaneously to prevent reinfection during the course of therapy. Since the organism is less likely to be transmitted homosexually among females, simultaneous treatment of asymptomatic female partners is not recommended but may be undertaken in the interest of caution.

How can you avoid trichomoniasis? ———————

As with N.S.V., a woman can minimize the risk of trichomoniasis by washing her hands before and after manual sex play and by avoiding the transfer of fluids from one vagina to another. If anorectal contact takes place, wash your hands (or other organ or instrument) before making contact with the vagina.

In heterosexual or male homosexual activity, transfer of the parasite can be prevented if the man wears a condom.

CHAPTER 7

Moniliasis

(Transmitted Homosexually among Men and Women)

What is it?

Moniliasis is an infection caused by a genus of yeast-like fungus called *Monilia* (also called *Candida albicans*). The infection is alternately named "thrush" and "candidiasis."

The fungus is a normal vaginal organism, present in small quantities in just about all women. An infection develops when there is a reduction in the natural flora that inhibit the fungus's growth.

Infection is especially prevalent in pregnancy, following the use of broad-spectrum antibiotics, and among diabetics. It also develops frequently among women who use oral contraceptives, which simulate the hormonal climate of pregnancy. Presumably all these conditions destroy or diminish the inhibiting flora.

Monilia infections also may develop in the mouth, urethra, or intestines, or in the moist area beneath the penile foreskin, or under the fingernails. Presumably they reach these sites initially as a result of vaginal contact. However, once there, they may be transmitted to another nonvaginal site. Thus, a man might acquire a monilia infection beneath the fingernails during a heterosexual encounter and transfer it to the rectum of another man, from whom a third man might acquire a urethral infection.

How do you know you have it?

In women, the chief symptom is a thin, cloudy, white vaginal discharge that may look or smell somewhat like cottage cheese.

The discharge is usually accompanied by itching. In uncircumcised men, pus or irritation may develop under the foreskin and will be especially profuse if the man is diabetic. The infection can also cause a watery urethral discharge and itchiness inside the urethra. When the infected site is other than the genitals, there usually are no symptoms.

How do you get it?

As has been noted, the infection results initially from suppression of natural vaginal bacterial flora. Thus, it can develop as a side effect of any condition that suppresses them, principal among which are those conditions listed above.

Women whose activity is exclusively homosexual generally do not take oral contraceptives and therefore are less likely to incur the infection than women who do. However, any woman can incur it as a result of contact with an infected partner.

The infectious fungus is rather hearty and can survive for minutes and sometimes even hours outside the warm, moist climes where it thrives. Thus, it can be passed among women who share towels, washcloths, clothing, or bedsheets.

Men whose activity is exclusively homosexual and who limit themselves to partners whose activity is exclusively homosexual will not ordinarily contract the infection by sexual transmission. They can, however, contract it nonsexually — though this is quite rare.

How is it diagnosed?

Diagnosis of moniliasis is made by examining the discharge under a microscope to observe the fungus. It may be necessary to grow a laboratory culture to demonstrate the fungus convincingly.

How is it treated?

In women, moniliasis can often be overcome without drugs. When symptoms appear, promptly douche once with a solution of one teaspoon vinegar in one quart of water. If this treatment is successful, symptoms should abate within two days. Meanwhile, you can relieve itching by applying a cold compress over the vulva, by sitting in a bath of cool water, or by pouring over the labia minora a solution of one-eighth cup baking soda in one quart of water.

If douching does not overcome the infection, the first choice of treatment is nystatin. The second choice of treatment, for women who have an allergy (very rare) to nystatin or who for some other reason have difficulty maintaining the preferred regimen, is douching with a solution of gentian or crystal violet. After the entire vagina has been cleansed and dried, apply the solution liberally to the external genitalia, particularly the clitoris and labia. Douche every third day until the infection subsides. However, douching should not be employed during pregnancy, for it may lead to fetal damage. In pregnancy-related infections, of course, the infection should subside after the baby is born.

The third choice of treatment is a propion gel vaginal suppository, administered twice daily for three weeks.

In diabetes and in pregnancy, unfortunately, the nystatin and propion gel sometimes prove unsuccessful. The only solution is to manage the infection — that is, minimize its discomforts — with topical techniques mentioned earlier.

If the infection is caused by oral contraceptives, the best solution often is to switch to another method of birth control. The infection should subside shortly after the pills are discontinued. Meanwhile, it can be managed with douching and other techniques.

If the infection appears to be a side effect of antibiotics, an alternate medication may be prescribed.

In men, treatment often is unnecessary. If there is not repeated exposure to an infected person, the infection will go away on its own. If the infection is under the foreskin, topical application of nystatin ointment is helpful. Apply the ointment liberally to the infected area daily until the infection subsides.

When a diabetic male has the infection under his foreskin, circumcision may be necessary, for this is the only way to remove the climate where the fungus thrives, namely, a dark, warm, moist area. Until circumcision is performed, relief can be obtained by applying a 2 percent solution of gentian violet daily for three days.

However, when a persistent discharge issues from beneath the foreskin, do not be content with a diagnosis of moniliasis. Test for gonorrhea, syphilis, and other serious sexually transmitted diseases. There is also the possibility of penile cancer. If the infection does not respond promptly to treatment for moniliasis, circumcision is virtually mandatory for diagnosis as well as for symptomatic relief.

How can you avoid moniliasis?

If the infection is related to oral contraceptives or antibiotics, the obvious way to avoid it in the future is to use other agents when available. In general, women might also do the following:

• Avoid perfumed douches. Chemicals in these preparations seem to destroy the vaginal flora that naturally suppress monilia. (Some physicians recommend not douching even with plain water except as treatment for specific conditions.)

• Do not douche too often. Frequency of greater than once a week can evacuate the vaginal flora that naturally suppress monilia.

• Wear cotton panties or none at all rather than those made of synthetic fibers. The latter do not ventilate well and create an atmosphere of warmth and moisture more hospitable to the development of the fungus.

• Wash your hands before manual sex play with another woman and avoid transferring the fluids of one vagina to another. If anorectal contact takes place, wash your hands (or other organ or instrument) before making contact with the vagina.

In heterosexual or male homosexual activity, transfer of infection can be prevented if the man wears a condom.

CHAPTER 8

Lymphogranuloma Venereum (L.G.V.)

(Transmitted Homosexually Almost Exclusively among Men)

With lymphogranuloma venereum, we return to those diseases that have serious consequences, like syphilis and gonorrhea, rather than those whose legacy is mere inconvenience. Though L.G.V. is rare — extremely rare outside the tropics — it can cause permanent disfigurement and great pain. It is highly contagious. Its rarity, in view of the ease of contagion, owes to the hideous swelling that occurs around the genitals of sufferers. If the swelling does not persuade the victim himself to refrain from sexual contact, it can scare off prospective partners.

What is L.G.V.?

It is an infection caused by a virus-like chlamydia organism, an agent of the psittacosis lymphogranuloma group. These organisms are larger than viruses and smaller than rickettsiae (which, in turn, are smaller than bacteria). They collect and multiply in the human lymph glands.

The disease was first reported medically in the eighteenth century. Early accounts noted that it was found only in the tropics and that it was characterized by swelling of the lymph glands of the groin, followed by discharge of pus through the skin. If untreated, these swellings would cause gross enlargement of the genitals and surrounding areas, including the thighs. These enlargements came to be called "elephantiasis."

How do you get it? ———————————————

Early diagnosticians speculated that the disease may have been transmitted by some sort of tropical insect, as was malaria. Later findings revealed that transmission was by human contact. Usually that contact proved to be genital-to-genital, but the infectious organism can also enter the body through the mouth, eye, or other organs. There are cases of surgeons contracting the disease after operating on an infected patient.

How do you know you have it? ———————————

The first symptom of L.G.V. usually is a pimple-like eruption on or near the genitals. It appears between seven days and four weeks after contact. It is generally accompanied by slight and painless swelling of the genitals themselves and/or of the surrounding skin.

If treatment is not instituted, the symptoms will often disappear. Meanwhile, two to seven days later, the lymph nodes in the groin swell. Usually this swelling is accompanied by discharge of pus through the skin. In addition, the skin surface may become grumous, that is, dotted with lumps whose tips appear scab-like.

If the disease still goes untreated, the symptoms worsen. The swelling may reach such proportions that there will appear to be growths the size of footballs beneath the skin. While this is happening on the outer surfaces of the body, there is parallel growth inside. The obstruction may press against the rectum or urethra, making defecation or urination difficult — and eventually impossible. At times, the throat may also be infected or the disease may invade the nervous system, causing chronic severe headaches.

These complications are not inevitable. In some cases, the symptoms will gradually subside and eventually vanish, with no recurrence or other problems. Much more often, however, there will be at least some permanent damage. If a urethral stricture has developed — that is, if the passageway has been narrowed by encroachment of the surrounding masses — a physician may have to dilate it with progressively larger rods, called "sounds," to restore the ability to urinate. The bulbous growths will usually have to be removed surgically.

There are, of course, other infections that may produce swelling of the genital region. Sometimes these infections, which are not transmitted by contact, may also produce some of the more advanced symptoms of L.G.V.

How is L.G.V. diagnosed?

Diagnosis is confirmed by one or more laboratory tests. The original test, no longer used in the United States, was developed in 1925 by venereologist Wilhelm Siegmund Frei. A specimen of pus is obtained from the infected person and is sterilized. The sterile material is then injected into the patient's skin. If L.G.V. is present, the area of injection will become red, hot, and swollen. This will happen within twenty-four to forty-eight hours of the injection, and will last from four to eight days.

Unfortunately, the patient remains sensitive to sterile pus for years and possibly for a lifetime. Thus, in future tests, a diagnostician cannot determine whether the patient has an early active stage of the disease or merely a sensitivity from previous infection.

A newer version of this same procedure, the Barnwell test, appears to produce permanent sensitivity less frequently than the Frei test. However, while this makes the test preferable, it is by no means foolproof. Secondary testing will usually be necessary to confirm the disease in someone believed to be reinfected.

One secondary vehicle is a complement-fixation tes of blood. The patient's serum is mixed with a material that represents the infection. If there is a reaction, the test is positive. However, while a negative result usually indicates reliably that the patient does not have L.G.V., a positive result is not foolproof confirmation of the disease.

Another secondary procedure is a biopsy of the tissue in the lymph nodes. Under a microscope, it may reveal development characteristic of L.G.V. Further identification of the infectious organism may be made by culturing a specimen of pus.

How is L.G.V. treated?

The treatment of choice is one of the sulfonamides in a three-week regimen. The patient should drink large quantities of water during this therapy — at least eight full ounces with each dose, and preferably an additional quart or two per day.

Second choice for patients who are allergic to or do not respond to the sulfonamides is doxycycline or minocycline. Third choice is tetracycline. In certain patients for whom none of the above regimens proved successful, success has been achieved with a combination of sulfisoxazole and tetracycline.

Supplementary treatment may be necessary, especially in advanced stages of the disease. If there are large quantities of pus in the swollen lymph nodes, a physician may have to pass a needle into the nodes and extract the pus before it breaks out through the skin. If the pus breaks out, infection will spread. Moreover, once the skin has broken, surgical removal of the pus (by a needle or other means) is dangerous; cutting into the area encourages development of a persistent draining tract.

If the disease has progressed to the stage where a rectal or urethral stricture occurs, dilatation will be necessary to stretch the passageway. More extensive surgery may be necessary if there is blockage of the intestinal tract. This surgery may involve removal of a portion of the intestine.

How can you avoid L.G.V.?

As with other diseases that are spread by contact, the best way to avoid the disease is to avoid contact with an infected person. The organisms of L.G.V. are harbored in the pus cells and would not be spread if they did not directly contact another person's body; thus, to use an exaggerated example for purposes of clarity, if your hair stylist happened to have L.G.V., you would not be likely to catch it simply from the type of contact that ordinarily takes place between stylist and customer — the contact of his hands and your head. However, if your skin was in some way brought into contact with the swollen areas of an L.G.V. victim's genital region, it is quite likely that you would be infected — especially if there has been discharge of pus. If you have contact with a person who is asymptomatic or whose infection is in such an early stage that significant swelling has not begun, it is extremely unlikely that you will contract the disease.

Unless you are in the tropics or have sex with someone who recently returned from the tropics, your chances of catching the disease are extremely slim. Of course, no matter where you are, if you notice swelling or ulceration in a prospective partner's genital area, ask what it is and whether he or she has had it diagnosed. If it isn't L.G.V., it could very well be some other contagious disease.

CHAPTER 9

Granuloma Inguinale

(Transmitted Homosexually among Men and Women)

Granuloma inguinale and lymphogranuloma venereum have a few similarities beyond that of their names. A granuloma is defined medically as a lesion (that is, a tissue abnormality) that (a) results from inflammation caused by a biologic, chemical, or physical agent; (b) is granule-like (that is, fairly well circumscribed and firmer than the uninvolved adjacent tissue); and (c) generally persists in the tissue as a chronic, slowly worsening inflammation. It usually involves accumulation of single-celled structures, called "phagocytes," at or near the site of infection. "Inguinale" refers to the groin — as "venereum" refers to the genital region in general.

Like L.G.V., granuloma inguinale involves swelling in the genital region, usually accompanied by ulceration. Also, it is found chiefly in the tropics and subtropics, and is spread by contact with infected skin surfaces or their pus. However, unlike L.G.V., granuloma inguinale does not lead to gross subdermal masses. Instead, the infected skin is destroyed and replaced by scar tissue.

Like L.G.V., granuloma inguinale is rare. Also, it is painful and can produce permanent skin disfigurement. However, it does not ordinarily cause damage to internal organs.

What is it?

The infectious organism in granuloma inguinale is believed to be the bacterium Donovania granulomatis, also known as "the Donovan body," after surgeon Charles Donovan, who discovered it in 1905. We say "believed to be" because these organisms are found when patients have the disease and are the means by which diagnosis is made, but researchers have not been able to produce the disease by transfer of the organisms, so the possibility exists that they are a by-product rather than a causative agent. In any case, their presence is a sure sign that lesions of the genital region are granuloma inguinale rather than some other disease.

How do you get it?

Granuloma inguinale is transferred by contact with the infected surface. The contact that most people report involves genital apposition, but the organism can also invade the skin of the mouth or lips and possibly the hands.

How do you know you have it?

The first symptom is usually a painless red swelling on the genitals, in the groin, or on the flesh that covers the pubic bone. It usually will appear from two to three months after contact. Thus, for a very long period after contracting the disease, you don't know you have it. There is some dispute as to whether the disease can be transmitted during this latent stage, but the possibility exists. Thus, once diagnosis has been confirmed, it is prudent to warn people who were partners during that period. If they do not develop symptoms, treatment is not necessary. However, if they do develop symptoms, the knowledge that you had granuloma inguinale can facilitate a partner's diagnosis.

Within three or four days after the initial appearance of the red swelling, the infected region expands. Then the granulomas develop — grain-like ulcers that take on a beef-red color and a thickness significantly greater than that of normal skin. Soon the red areas give way to scar tissue. In some cases, infection develops atop the scar tissue, producing further ulceration, which in turn may lead to development of another layer of scar tissue.

Many other complications can ensue. The scar tissue can eat away at the perineum (that is, the small section of flesh between the anus and the genitals). In women, the deterioration can lead to a hole between the rectum and the vagina; the destroyed area will then have to be reconstructed with flesh taken from elsewhere on the body. In men, scar tissue can cause the urethra to be narrowed or strictured. The lymph nodes themselves will not swell, as in L.G.V.; however, the scar tissue of granuloma inguinale can block the lymph passageways, causing the genitals themselves to swell.

If the disease goes untreated, in addition to scarring the genital region irreparably, it can lead to general body weakness, which renders the victim more susceptible to all infection.

How is it diagnosed?

Diagnosis generally is made by inspection — the appearance of the lesions is unique — and confirmed by laboratory identification of Donovan bodies on a smear taken from a granuloma. Further confirmation can come from biopsy of the edge of a granuloma: many plasma cells are seen, a sign of this particular type of chronic infection.

How is granuloma inguinale treated?

The preferred treatment is doxycycline hyclate; a second choice is minocycline. For patients who are allergic or do not respond to these regimens, the treatment is tetracycline. Supplementary treatment in advanced stages of the disease may include surgical removal of scar tissue, repair of a damaged perineum or rectovaginal wall, or sounding of a strictured urethra.

How can you avoid granuloma inguinale? ——————

As with L.G.V., the disease can be avoided if you avoid tactile contact with an infected person. While it is uncertain whether the disease can be transmitted by an asymptomatic carrier, the overwhelming majority of reports involve contact with symptomatic people. More specifically, reported transmission almost inevitably involves contact with the infected tissue itself, not merely with some other part of the body of an infected person.

If you notice swelling or ulceration in a prospective partner's genital area — or anything else unusual — ask what it is and whether he or she has had it diagnosed. If it isn't granuloma inguinale, it could very well be some other contagious disease.

CHAPTER 10

Chancroid

(Transmitted Homosexually among Men and Women)

What is it?

Like L.G.V. and granuloma inguinale, chancroid is a local disease. That is, it infects a certain area of the body and remains there or spreads only to surrounding areas; it does not (like syphilis or gonorrhea) spread through the bloodstream to distant organs.

The causative organism is the bacillus (a form of bacteria) hemophilus ducreyi, also called "Ducrey's bacillus," after dermatologist Augusto Ducrey, who identified it in 1889. The disease itself has existed since ancient times but was not recognized as a separate entity until the past century; previously, it was mistaken for syphilis.

The chancre from which "chancroid" derives its name is identical in appearance to that of syphilis. The difference is in the texture. The chancre of syphilis, when examined with a gloved hand (gloved so that the examiner does not contract the disease), has the firm feel of a piece of "index stock," the kind of paper often used for business cards; the chancre of chancroid has a soft consistency.

There is another significant difference between the two chancres. That of syphilis generally is painless, while that of chancroid usually is quite painful.

Chancroid is, like L.G.V. and granuloma inguinale, regarded as a tropical disease. However, it can be transmitted in colder climes. How long an untreated person will remain contagious in colder areas is open to question. Lacking evidence to the contrary, the safest course is to assume he or she will be contagious indefinitely.

Unlike L.G.V. and granuloma inguinale, chancroid is not rare. In some countries it is estimated to account for 10 percent of all V.D. patients. In certain areas of the world, it is more common than either gonorrhea (the worldwide champion among serious venereal diseases) or syphilis (the second most prevalent).

How do you get it?

Because Ducrey's bacillus is relatively fragile and thrives only in moist human environments, transmission usually requires direct contact between the chancre and a mucous membrane. However, there have been cases of transmission to a diagnostician's finger or on an infected surgical dressing or towel.

Many medical texts report that chancroid is particularly prevalent under unsanitary living conditions. Whether these conditions foster nongenital transmission or whether it just happens that there is widespread squalor in the tropical areas where chancroid is most prevalent remains open to question. In any case, as with syphilis and gonorrhea, an asymptomatic carrier can transmit the disease.

How do you know you have it?

Three to seven days after transmission, a small red spot appears on the skin. Usually this will be the skin of the genitals, but the site may also be the anus, perineum, groin, or mouth.

The spot swells, then the skin becomes soft and ulcerates, producing a discharge. There can be any number of these red areas simultaneously or consecutively. The ulcers that develop have a rough surface and irregular edges, like the chancres of syphilis; but as has been noted, the chancre of syphilis generally is painless, while that of chancroid usually is quite painful. Also, when touched, the chancre of chancroid bleeds easily; that of syphilis does not.

If treatment is not undertaken, the chancre expands. If this takes place in the genital area, it usually blocks the lymph nodes, which become swollen and painful. If treatment still is not initiated, a pus-like substance develops, the skin breaks, and the pus-like substance begins to drain. Areas of skin onto which it drains now ulcerate, and eventually the infected region is covered with large raw surfaces like those in granuloma inguinale.

How is chancroid diagnosed?

Diagnosis generally is made by inspection and confirmed by laboratory examination of smears from the chancre. When stained, these reveal small red rods that differ considerably from the fragile spirochete of syphilis (which, it will be recalled, can ordinarily be viewed only through a dark-field microscope). If these "rods" — more precisely, colonies of *Hemophilus ducreyi* — are not immediately apparent, cultures can be grown on special media and incubated for two or three days, after which the "rods" almost inevitably appear if chancroid is present.

When diagnosis is difficult on the basis of a smear, a biopsy of the edge of the ulcer can be taken and examined microscopically. Another, older method for confirming diagnosis involves injection into the skin of a testing material that produces swelling in infected patients. However, the test is rarely used these days because it produces both false negatives and false positives.

Chancroid and syphilis can occur at the same time, so it is extremely important to confirm or eliminate each diagnosis. To reiterate, a confirmed diagnosis of chancroid does not rule out syphilis, nor does a confirmed diagnosis of syphilis rule out chancroid. Syphilis, of course, is more dangerous than chancroid; thus, even if a diagnosis of syphilis cannot be confirmed, it is advisable to follow a patient with monthly blood tests for a minimum of three months and preferably for six months. In advanced stages of chancroid, when swelling and/or reddening of skin takes place, further testing is advisable to rule out L.G.V. and granuloma inguinale.

How is chancroid treated?

The preferred treatment is one of the sulfonamides in a three-week regimen. Second choice for patients who are allergic to or do not respond to the sulfonamides is doxycycline or minocycline. Third choice is tetracycline.

Sexual relations should be avoided until chancroid is cured.

How can you avoid chancroid?

As with syphilis and other venereal diseases that can be transmitted by asymptomatic carriers, the only foolproof way to avoid chancroid is to avoid sexual relations with anyone who might have it — in other words, limit yourself to one partner who also limits himself or herself to you, and make sure that neither of you is infected when your relationship begins. Impractical though this may be, sex under other circumstances does involve the risk of chancroid (and syphilis and gonorrhea and other venereal diseases), and the risk increases in direct proportion to your number of partners and their number of partners.

A condom will offer some protection, but there are cases of chancroid transmission even when a condom was worn. Of course, if your partner has an open sore, particularly in the area of the genitals, the likelihood is much greater that you will contract chancroid or some other venereal disease. If you notice any genital irregularity in a prospective partner, by all means ask what it is and whether he or she has had it diagnosed.

CHAPTER 11

Viral Hepatitis

(Transmitted Homosexually among Men and Women)

Viral hepatitis may well become the most serious of all sexually transmissible diseases. It can kill or permanently disable you. If it doesn't, it can still put you out of commission for weeks. At its mildest, it can be an enervating and lingering illness.

Most people do not think of viral hepatitis as venereal. There are, of course, nonsexual ways to contract the disease. However, recent research indicates that sexual transmission and especially homosexual transmission are far more prevalent than ever suspected. A study at the Lindsley F. Kimball Research Institute of the New York Blood Center revealed that 5 to 7 percent of a test group of homosexually active men had within their blood a material that probably was the virus, while 50 to 60 percent showed a blood reaction indicating that the virus was once present. The percentages among men whose activity was exclusively heterosexual were only a small fraction of these figures.

What is viral hepatitis? ———————————————

Hepatitis is inflammation of the liver. The word's roots are *hepar*, liver, and the medical suffix for inflammation, *itis*. The liver may become inflamed in a variety of ways: ingestion of poison, longtime heavy consumption of alcohol, and infection are three of the most common.

Viral hepatitis is infection by a virus (as opposed to a bacterium or other organism). Researchers divide these infections into two types whose names are somewhat misleading. There is Type A viral hepatitis, usually called "infectious hepatitis." It is indeed infectious, but so is the other type: Type B, usually called "serum hepatitis." This name derives from the fact that Type B is commonly transmitted in blood transfusions or on contaminated hypodermic needles.

Note well: Type B is infectious. Awareness of its infectious character and of means of transmission other than through the bloodstream has led to its acquiring the additional names, "Australia Antigen Hepatitis" and "Hepatitis B/Genital." Don't trouble yourself trying to keep track of these names now; think only in terms of "Type A" and "Type B." The other names will fall neatly into place later in the chapter.

"A" and "B" are two distinct kinds of infection. They are not simply the same infection transmitted by different routes; they appear to be distinct disease entities, caused by different viruses. Despite many research advances in the past few years, scientists still have only a general idea of the various properties of the two types. What follows here is a summary of the conclusions most widely accepted at this time. It is hoped the not too distant future will see a clarification and resolution of many uncertainties.

Type A viral hepatitis is by far the less dangerous of the two. It has a mortality rate of about 2 per 1,000 cases — as contrasted to a rate of about 11 percent, or 110 per 1,000, with certain varieties of Type B.

Hepatitis A has been recognized for two centuries. It has been called "epidemic jaundice" and "catarrhal jaundice" as well as "infectious hepatitis." The names tell us something about the history of the disease.

The virus that transmits Hepatitis A thrives in the human intestinal tract. It is passed in the feces of an infected person. It accumulates in contaminated water. It then may be ingested by people who drink the water or who eat raw shellfish that inhabited the water. It may also be carried directly to the mouth on contaminated fingers, by analingus, or by a variety of other vehicles. It has the ability to survive the acids of the stomach, which kill many harmful bacteria and viruses. It then passes into the liver, causing inflammation. Some people who develop hepatitis become jaundiced — that is, their skin and the whites of their eyes take on a yellowish hue.

Historically, Hepatitis A has most frequently occurred in epidemics. Hence, the name "epidemic jaundice." One of its symptoms may be the coughing up of mucus, also called catarrh; hence, "catarrhal jaundice."

It is not surprising that the disease frequently appears in epidemics. If a body of drinking water is contaminated — as, for example, when a sewer line leaks into a supply of drinking water — everyone who drinks is exposed. If a body of contaminated water contains clams, oysters or other shellfish that are eaten raw, everyone who eats them is exposed. Indeed, public health officials find that it is much easier to trace a large epidemic of Hepatitis A to its source than to trace a few scattered cases. Frequently with epidemics, the sufferers have been living under conditions that are easily recognizable as unsanitary: for example, campers using an open ditch latrine that is not far from a stream that produced drinking water.

Not everyone who is exposed to the virus catches the disease, and not everyone who catches the disease develops symptoms. Thus, in a typical region where an epidemic has occurred, there will be an uninfected group of people, an infected group with symptoms, and an infected group without symptoms. The latter group is the most dangerous because its members can transmit the disease to huge numbers of people without ever realizing they are doing so.

Obviously, sexual transmission of Hepatitis A is not limited to homosexually active people. The disease can be transmitted in heterosexual or homosexual analingus. It can be transmitted in heterosexual or homosexual penis-anus penetration if the contaminated partner's penis transfers the virus to either partner's hands and if the hands transfer it to the noninfected partner's mouth, or if there is direct contact between the contaminated penis and the mouth, or if the virus is transferred from penis to one mouth to another mouth. The virus is hardy and can survive numerous transfers. Indeed, it may even be taken in the mouth during heterosexual or homosexual cunnilingus or fellatio if the recipient of these ministrations happens to have been less than fastidious after defecating; the moist or semimoist warmth of the groin is a particularly hospitable nesting place for germs of this sort. However, the virus probably cannot be contracted directly through the penis during anal intercourse; it apparently cannot enter the liver except through the digestive tract.

Hepatitis B was identified in 1883 and called "serum hepatitis," "homologous serum jaundice," or "transfusion hepatitis." The names testify to the then-prevailing belief that the virus could be transmitted only through the blood. Remember, this is *not* the same virus as in Hepatitis A, which inhabits the intestinal tract. The theory was that this other virus — the Type B virus — went directly from bloodstream to bloodstream, transmitted during a transfusion from an infected person or during an injection made by a needle that previously had been used on an infected person. The medical term for this mode of transmission is "parenteral," meaning not through the alimentary canal but rather by injection through the skin ("subcutaneous"), into a muscle ("intramuscular"), or into a vein ("intravenous").

The theory of parenteral transmission was not erroneous, only incomplete. The fact is, many if not most symptomatic cases of Hepatitis B are transmitted by transfusion (with the blood coming from a blood bank that pays donors) or by unsanitary injection (especially among narcotics users sharing a hypodermic needle).

The prevalence of Hepatitis B in these two situations suggests a scenario revolving around narcotics users. One of them has the disease and transmits it to others on a shared needle. It enters the blood of all members of the group. Some of these members sell blood to help support their habit. There is further spread of the disease. Those who contract it tend to be individuals who must use blood from a bank that buys it rather than one that accepts only less-likely-to-be-contaminated donated blood. Narcotics users tend to be such people. Thus, the circle broadens — and the more people within it who contract Hepatitis B, the more likely that others will contract it.

To repeat, it was for many years believed that Hepatitis B could be transmitted *only* in this way. Indeed, as recently as 1974, the author of a book on venereal disease advised: "The virus of serum hepatitis, while causing the same disease pattern as that of infectious hepatitis, can only get to the liver by being injected into the flesh (and hence the bloodstream) by a needle or sharp instrument recently used by a person who is already developing hepatitis." But the evidence now at hand reveals that this is not true. Hepatitis B apparently can be transmitted also by ingesting the saliva or semen of an infected person.

The first step in understanding these new dimensions of Hepatitis B was taken in 1965, when oncologist — and 1976 Nobel laureate — Baruch S. Blumberg of the Institute for Cancer Research at Philadelphia found certain particles in the blood of diseased patients. He reported the particles as "the Australian antigen," an infectious agent previously not associated with hepatitis. But he had seen only the shell, not the oyster: the Australian antigen proved to be the covering of the actual virus, now called "the Dane particle," identified in 1970 by English pathologist David M. S. Dane.

Dane made another discovery: when a person has symptomatic Hepatitis B, the blood contains enormous quantities of the virus: as many as 10^{12} particles. Usually patients with viral diseases have very few particles except when they are acutely ill, and even then the numbers are much smaller than these.

The discoveries of Blumberg and Dane made it possible to determine by blood tests not only whether a person now has the virus but also whether that person ever had it. Tests were conducted with several thousand blood donors. The results were revealing. In the total population of volunteer blood donors, approximately .2 percent (or two donors per 1,000) were asymptomatic carriers. But among heavy narcotics users, 5 percent (five per *hundred*) were asymptomatic carriers. In other words, heavy narcotics users were twenty-five times more likely (1 out of 20 versus 1 out of 500) to be carriers of Hepatitis B than people who were not heavy users.

This is consistent with previous theories about Hepatitis B being transmitted on narcotics users' needles. However, hematologist Wolf Szmuness of the Lindsley F. Kimball Research Institute of the New York Blood Center tested seven hundred homosexually active males for Hepatitis B. He found that 6 percent had a material in their bloodstream that probably constituted a "carrier level" of the Dane virus, while 55 percent had a blood reaction that indicated subcarrier levels — in other words, they had been exposed at one time to a carrier, even though they may not have absorbed sufficient quantities of the virus to become carriers themselves.

In sum, the homosexually active group was *even more likely than the group of heavy narcotics users* to be asymptomatic carriers of Hepatitis B (6 percent versus 5 percent), and *more than half the entire group* apparently had been exposed at least once to the virus.

Dr. Szmuness did further studies in which presence of the virus correlated positively both to number of recent partners (the average of partners during the past six months in the homosexually active group was ten) and to a history of venereal disease. Such men might weigh this possibility and perhaps discuss it with a blood center physician before deciding to give blood.

The political aspects of this notwithstanding — we can appreciate the outrage of homosexually active males who deem themselves victims of statistical generalization — the significant medical inference is that these homosexually active possessors of the Dane particle evidently got it from somewhere other than blood transfusions and hypodermic needles. That inference led to a hypothesis which, under further laboratory testing, yielded the conclusion that the Dane particle is present in the saliva and semen as well as the blood. Sexual transmission can take place if either is ingested.

The implications of this conclusion are extremely serious. Aside from the dangers of hepatitis itself, there is an indication that the Hepatitis B virus may encourage cancer of the liver. Dr. Blumberg has reported that in West Africa, of twenty-four patients with a primary type of liver cancer, some twenty-one had bloodstream evidence of prior infection with Hepatitis B. There are, to be sure, many possible explanations for this correlation; nonetheless, if the potential exists for the Hepatitis B virus to cause or encourage cancer of the liver, then the presence of this virus in as many as 60 percent of the homosexually active population presents a potential public health problem of unforeseen magnitude.

Now, granted, the outcome of these statistics need not be bleak. Conceivably, the presence of the virus in so large a portion of the population may have the salubrious effect of vaccination. Just as the injection of a small quantity of the smallpox bacillus serves to prevent later contraction of the full-scale disease, so too may the relatively low levels of Hepatitis B among homosexually active males serve to inoculate them against disabling or even deadly episodes of viral hepatitis. At the same time, we cannot overlook the negative side of the situation. It may very well be that up to 60 percent of the homosexually active population comprises candidates for fatal cancer of the liver.

Can homosexually active people avoid the Hepatitis B virus? If a fellator — or fellatrice — has a variety of partners and ingests their semen, the odds are decidedly against it. Startling? Yes, but inescapable. The simple fact is, if Hepatitis B is transmitted in the semen and even the saliva — as the evidence strongly suggests — and if you consume either of these substances, your chances of harboring the Dane particle (and the potential to carry Hepatitis B) are very, very good. This applies heterosexually as well as homosexually, but it is particularly significant homosexually because of the disproportionate number of homosexually active people who have been shown to harbor the virus.

Would a condom prevent transmission during fellatio? The question cannot be answered on the basis of current knowledge. However, we conjecture that the Hepatitis B virus is so small — 42 nanomillimeters — one nanomillimeter being 10^{-3} of a millimeter — that it would pass unobstructed through the walls of a condom.

The ideal solution to the problem would be a vaccine. Quite possibly, as noted above, the presence of the virus itself — in subclinical quantities — may serve as one. Meanwhile, pediatrician Saul Krugman of the New York University School of Medicine has developed a compound which, in future tests, may serve to vaccinate against Hepatitis B. At present, however, the disease looms as one of the most serious dangers of homosexual intercourse, especially — though certainly not exclusively — among men.

How do you know you have viral hepatitis? —————

The early symptoms of viral hepatitis, whether Type A or Type B, are nonspecific and common to many diseases. Victims lose their appetite, tire easily, feel feverish, and become nauseated. In addition, there may be pain in the joints, a cough, a sore throat, and pain or a feeling of fullness in the upper right quadrant of the abdomen. Not surprisingly, many victims believe they are "coming down with the flu" or suffering some other form of general infection. Among cigarette smokers, a "bad taste" may develop.

In Hepatitis A, these symptoms generally appear between fifteen and sixty days after the disease is contracted. In Hepatitis B, they usually appear between sixty and one hundred eighty days after the infectious contact.

After several days of these symptoms, the urine may darken to the color of a cola soft drink and the feces may become light reddish-brown, like clay. This is the result of liver malfunction. About one to four days later, jaundice develops. It begins with a yellowing of the sclera ("whites" of the eyes). Then the entire skin takes on a yellowish cast.

How is hepatitis diagnosed? —————

Whether or not jaundice develops, diagnosis of hepatitis A or B is confirmed by discovery of the relevant virus in laboratory tests of the blood serum. If jaundice does not develop, the disease will frequently go undetected — but the victim may remain a carrier indefinitely.

How is it treated?

There is no known treatment for either variety of hepatitis. If the victim feels weary or has other symptoms of infection, bed rest is encouraged. In any case, physical exertion should be avoided, for it may strain the body and impede recovery. Alcohol should not be consumed, for it can damage the liver. Hepatoxic drugs (that is, those which can damage a vulnerable liver) should also be avoided. Chief among them is morphine sulfate. Small doses of barbiturates may be safe, but the safer course is to avoid them entirely.

In severe cases, vomiting may be considerable and/or the person may go into a coma or semicoma. Hospitalization will permit intravenous feeding, enforced bed rest, and constant medical monitoring. Hepatic coma or dehydration due to vomiting can, if not promptly treated, prove fatal.

If nausea and vomiting are significant problems, or if oral intake is substantially decreased (either due to coma or semicoma or simple lack of appetite), the preferred treatment is intravenous administration of a 10 percent glucose solution. If there are signs of impending coma, protein should be withheld, then gradually introduced and increased as clinical improvement takes place.

Generally, the jaundice phase of the disease will last about six to eight weeks, although in some cases it will end in as few as three weeks. When the jaundice passes, victims normally feel much better, but they usually do not feel fully recovered for three to four months.

Sufferers remain infectious at least until the jaundice phase has ended and often for some months beyond. Until laboratory tests reveal that levels of the infectious virus have receded, victims of the disease should use only their own towels, utensils, dishes, clothing, etc. People who have been or will be in close contact with the infected person should be given an injection of gamma globulin before or as soon as possible after exposure to prevent the disease from gaining a foothold. The more time that passes after exposure, the less effective the gamma globulin treatment will be. Five or six weeks after exposure, it is unlikely to be helpful.

Hepatitis tends to be more severe and dangerous in the elderly or those with other complicating illnesses. Overall mortality for Hepatitis A is under 1 percent, but mortality appears to be closer to 2 percent over age fifty. Particularly vulnerable, it seems, are postmenopausal women.

Mortality is somewhat more difficult to assess for Hepatitis B, since so many people have the disease asymptomatically. Among people who were contaminated parenterally, the mortality rate appears to be 10 to 12 percent. Among others, it probably is about the same as for Hepatitis A.

While a gamma globulin injection usually will prevent development of Hepatitis B if administered before or shortly after exposure, the short-range effectiveness of the injection, coupled with autoimmunity and other factors, makes a program of gamma globulin prophylaxis impractical. However, studies now are under way involving prophylactic injection of a special preparation containing substances from the blood of people who have subclinical levels of the disease. One of the largest scale studies of this sort, funded by Ortho Diagnostics, is being carried out at the Howard Brown Memorial Clinic in Chicago. People who would like to participate or who seek more information about the study should contact the Brown clinic or Ortho Diagnostics, Raritan, N.J. 08869.

How can you avoid hepatitis?

Since Hepatitis A is carried in the feces, chances of contracting it are enhanced when there is fecal or anorectal contact. Analingus is especially likely to transmit infection, but the virus can also be transmitted indirectly — if, for example, fellatio is performed on a penis that has not been washed thoroughly after anal intercourse, or if the virus is carried to the mouth on the hands after touching the anus, the recently-withdrawn penis, or some other contaminated surface.

If one avoids analingus and thoroughly washes the penis and

hands following penetration, the likelihood of Hepatitis A is reduced but not eliminated. This hardy virus will often withstand even the most vigorous scrubbing with antiseptic soap.

There is no known way at present to protect oneself against Hepatitis B, short of avoiding sexual contact with a carrier of the disease — a difficult task for the nonmonogamous, since carriers often are asymptomatic. Researchers are at work on developing a vaccine.

CHAPTER 12

Amebiasis and Shigellosis

(Transmitted Homosexually Chiefly among Men)

While Hepatitis A is probably the most serious disease that can be transmitted through oral-fecal contact, it is by no means the only one. Two others, virtually identical in basic character and mode of transmission, are amebiasis and shigellosis. Because of their similarities, we will consider them here as a unit.

What are amebiasis and shigellosis?

Amebiasis is an infection caused by the protozoon entamoeba histolytica. (Amebae and protozoa are, strictly speaking, different classes of one-celled animals; the name amebiasis is technically a misnomer.) The organisms reside in the intestine, sometimes in the lining of the bowel but more often in the just-developed feces in the region of the colon. As the feces pass down into the rectum, most organisms move up into the newly forming replacement feces of the colon, but some are passed from the body in the feces. These promptly go into a dormant stage. If not returned to a human environment, they eventually die. However, if they are ingested, they pass through the stomach and revivify in the intestine. Now they are capable of reproducing (by cell division, as with all single-celled organisms). The human who becomes the new host of the organisms then is capable of passing their offspring on to someone else — while, of course, retaining a full complement in his or her own intestine.

Amebiasis — also called amebic dysentery — is particularly prevalent in the tropics. Incidence of infection in the United States is estimated at 2 to 5 percent of the total population. However, most infected people show no sign of the disease, because the amebae do not infect the lining of the person's bowel; they simply reside in the feces. When the amebae do infect the lining of the bowel — and especially of the colon — small ulcers are formed and symptoms appear. The usual primary symptom is a siege of intermittent constipation and diarrhea, sometimes accompanied by spots of blood or pus in the feces. Defecation may be painful. The victim may also suffer abdominal cramps and frequent episodes of flatus.

Inconvenient though these symptoms are, they usually do not create a serious health problem. However, occasionally the ulcers may permit amebae to enter the bloodstream and travel to the liver, where they can develop into abscesses (swollen pockets of dead liver tissue containing amebae and waste fluids). If these abscesses go untreated, the victim usually develops high fever. Over a period of time there will generally be a considerable loss of weight. A common symptom during this period is profuse perspiration while sleeping. Characteristically, the symptoms come and go: a person will feel normal for several weeks, then get another siege of symptoms, then feel normal again, then get symptoms again.

In rare cases, a liver abscess will rupture. This can lead to serious and possibly fatal damage to the liver, lungs, bloodstream, or other vital organs or systems. This is extremely rare and generally transpires only in very advanced stages of the disease.

The chief difference between amebiasis and shigellosis is that the infectious agent in the latter (also called bacillary dysentery) is not a protozoan but a bacterium, *Shigella*, a genus of the tribe Salmonella. The symptoms are virtually interchangeable, except that shigellosis usually does not provoke episodes of flatus. There is no liver involvement and consequently no serious threat to vital systems; however, if untreated for a prolonged period, shigellosis can produce high fevers and other traits of serious infection and can, in extreme cases, lead to fatal complications.

How do you get these diseases? ────────────

They are transmitted through oral-fecal contact. This may be direct, as in analingus, or indirect, as when oral contact is made with a contaminated penis or fingers. The organisms are hearty and may remain alive for a considerable period in food, water, and other media. Thus, nonsexual transmission is also possible — and indeed occurs quite frequently, especially in unhygienic environments.

How do you know you have them? ──────────────

The symptoms described above are quite similar to a variety of intestinal disorders, including certain kinds of food poisoning. Preliminary diagnosis is made by exclusion: What did the victim eat? Under what circumstances? Did others eat the same foods? If identical symptoms are reported by a large number of people in identical circumstances — for instance, soldiers in a given platoon, students at a certain fraternity house — the likelihood is that the infection was transmitted in food or the water supply. If symptoms are experienced by only one person, and if there is a history of anorectal contact, the hypothesis is that transmission was sexual.

How are amebiasis and shigellosis diagnosed? ─────

Diagnosis is confirmed by microscopic examination of the victim's feces. Often several stool specimens will have to be examined before the organisms can be identified. There are several blood tests that can offer further confirmation, but none is completely reliable or routinely available.

If the disease has reached an advanced stage — especially if amebiasis has reached the point of liver involvement — diagnosis can be quite difficult, for a great many other disorders present the same general symptomatology.

How are these diseases treated?

Both respond well to a variety of antiparasitic drugs. Treatment of choice for both is metronidazole. Second choice is diiodohydroxyquin.

Both diseases seem to come quickly under control. However, with amebiasis, relapses sometimes occur months after treatment. It is a good idea to examine one stool every month for four months before considering the disease cured.

How can these diseases be avoided?

Sexual transmission of amebiasis and shigellosis can be avoided if oral-fecal contact is avoided. This means abstaining from analingus and avoiding secondary modes of transmission, as on the hands or penis.

Even if analingus does not take place, it is possible for the infectious organisms to be ingested if the testicles, perineum, or other parts of the body are licked and happen to have some organisms on them. The organisms could have gotten there during defecation, especially if the area was not thoroughly cleansed afterward. Physicians advise not merely wiping the anus after defecation but washing the entire region if oral sexual contact is going to take place.

Of course, the diseases can also be transmitted nonsexually, so the fact that you acquire one does not necessarily mean that your most recent partner or partners were infected. You might simply be the victim of unhygienic conditions in a restaurant or a polluted water supply. However, once you contract either disease, you are likely to transmit it to future sexual partners who perform analingus on you or who have other anorectal contact with you. It is prudent, therefore, to avoid exposing partners to contamination in any way until the disease is treated and follow-up testing reveals that there are no more organisms in your stools.

CHAPTER 13

Other Diseases that Result from Fecal Contamination

(Transmitted Homosexually Exclusively among Men)

While amebiasis and shigellosis appear to be the only diseases transmitted through oral-fecal contact, other infections can result from rectal intromission by the penis.

The bacterium escherichia coli is a natural resident of the large intestine and an important agent in the digestive process. It helps synthesize certain vitamins and also protects the body from various foreign bacteria that pass through the intestine. However, it is not entirely benign. Ingested, it can create considerable gastrointestinal distress. Indeed, the presence of escherichia coli in food or water is used as an index to the degree of fecal contamination of that food or water. This is true not only when the feces are infected by a foreign organism, as with amebiasis and shigellosis; it is true in all circumstances — and it was the discovery a century ago of the role of escherichia coli in dysentery that led to the sanitation practices that have made epidemics of dysentery virtually nonexistent in the industrial world today.

It is extremely rare for significant amounts of escherichia coli to enter the body as a result of oral-anorectal contact. The highest concentrations of the bacteria are in the midportion of the intestine (the ileocecal valve area). The tongue does not reach this area, and while there are additional concentrations in the rectum itself, it appears that only rarely if ever are sufficient quantities ingested to create a problem.

However, the bacterium can do considerable damage when it enters the urethra — even in small quantities. In the chapter on nonspecific urethritis we discussed complications involving the urethra itself. In addition to these complications, or sometimes without actually infecting the urethra, the bacterium can affect other organs. The following are some of the complications that may ensue:

Prostatitis

While most escherichia coli bacteria will be absorbed by the glands that line the urethra, some may make their way upward into the labyrinth of tubes and spaces surrounding the prostate gland. The result is inflammation of the prostate (prostatitis). Once inflamed, the gland swells. It is shaped rather like a doughnut, surrounding the urethra. As the inner circumference swells, it narrows the urethra, making urination difficult and painful. As the outer portion swells, it puts pressure on the rectum, creating a feeling of fullness, as if one had to defecate. Constipation and/or rectal pain may ensue.

The inflammation can develop into an abscess, causing great pain and possibly transmitting infection to other abdominal organs, or it can develop into a chronic infection that resists treatment or recurs regularly after what appears to be adequate therapy.

Treatment of prostatitis is complicated and tricky. In addition to treating the inflamed gland itself, the physician must treat attending symptoms: fever, chills, pain, and sometimes hasty ejaculation (caused by interference with the functioning of the ejaculatory ducts and other organs involved with the prostate in producing and expelling semen). Treatment inevitably is with antibiotics after cultures determine the drug to which the bacteria respond. This is done by testing the expressed prostatic detritus against a number of antibiotics. The antibiotic or antibiotics that prevent the growth of the bacteria in the culture should also cure the prostatic infection.*

---

*For more on prostatic problems, consult our book, *Your Prostate: What It Is, What It Does, and the Diseases That Affect It*, published by Doubleday in 1973.

Pyelonephritis

Whether or not escherichia coli bacteria invade the prostate, some organisms can continue upward into the kidneys, causing pyelonephritis. This very serious disease can actually destroy the kidneys and is probably the cause of many deaths due to kidney failure, although it is not always diagnosed as such at the time.

The chief symptoms of pyelonephritis are severe back pain, chills, fever, burning on urination, frequent urination, and pus in the urine. Bacteria other than escherichia coli can also cause pyelonephritis, and the source of the disease often is extremely difficult to determine.

As with prostatitis, treatment is with antibiotics, the specific agents being selected in a culture study.

Epididymitis

The epididymides (singular: epididymis) are flask-like structures immediately above the testicles. They store sperm cells until ejaculation is imminent, whereupon they propel these cells through the vasa deferentia to the trigone area outside the prostate gland, where the cells are combined with semen and other products of the ejaculate.

Occasionally escherichia coli, having reached the area of the prostate, will move down one or both vasa deferentia to the epididymides, producing inflammation. The condition is termed epididymitis. The usual primary symptom is swelling of the scrotum, which generally will feel hot, painful, and tender. Chills and fever may also occur, along with the general symptoms of any infection (tiredness, weakness, nausea, headache).

As with prostatitis and pyelonephritis, a number of bacteria can produce the infection. Thus diagnosis is difficult. Moreover, since there is no way of expressing material from the epididymides for a culture study, choice of antibiotics is largely a matter of choosing a wide-spectrum drug and hoping it works.

If it doesn't, another is tried, then another, until one is found that does work. Sometimes escherichia coli will appear in the urine, or epididymitis may occur simultaneously with escherichia coli–related prostatitis or urethritis, thus encouraging the conclusion that the same bacterium is responsible. However, epididymitis may also develop independently of other genitourinary disorder.

Even though treatment may appear to be adequate, epididymitis can recur and develop into a chronic infection. It is one of the very most painful disorders of the genitourinary system, and when a chronic infection develops, victims often live in dread of the next recurrence.

In extreme cases, surgery will be necessary to relieve the infection. The surgeon literally cuts away the infected surfaces inside the scrotum. Painful and expensive though surgery is, many patients state they would rather undergo surgery than continue to suffer the pain of chronic epididymitis.

Infection of the Skin of the Penis

The human skin usually is very resistant to infection. However, occasionally acute or chronic infections of the skin of the penis will develop in men who have performed rectal intromission.

In acute infections, the skin becomes red, hot, swollen, tender, and painful. Chronic infections are of a lower grade and may persist for a number of months. Generally they begin as a reddened area of irritation that eventually develops a superficial collection of pus and then a small ulcerated area.

Left untreated, these infections may go away on their own, but they may also worsen. Treatment, as with most bacterial infections, is with antibiotics. The specific agents are determined in a culture study.

Rectally Transmitted Tuberculosis

We are not aware of cases of tuberculosis where rectum-to-penis transmission has been established beyond doubt. However, as urologist John K. Lattimer demonstrated in 1954, vagina-to-penis transmission definitely is possible. If the tuberculum bacillus (the infectious agent in tuberculosis) can pass from the vagina to the penis, it almost certainly can also pass from the rectum to the penis. Indeed, the atmosphere of the intestine and the rectum is better suited to the bacillus' growth, and thus rectal transmission is probably more likely than vaginal transmission.

How can these conditions be avoided?

The condom can prevent escherichia coli bacteria from entering the urethra and from making contact with the skin of the penis. Naturally, if the bacteria do not enter the urethra, they cannot make their way to the prostate, kidneys, epididymides, or other internal organs. Almost certainly the condom can also prevent the tuberculum bacillus from entering the urethra.

Some writers have suggested that urinating and washing the penis immediately after rectal withdrawal will expel all harmful bacteria. There is reason to doubt this. Washing may prevent infection of the skin of the penis — which is relatively rare, anyway. However, the delicate lining of the urethra could absorb bacteria before urination could expel them. In any case, men have contracted escherichia coli urethral infection despite prompt post-withdrawal washing and urinating.

CHAPTER 14

Congestive Prostatitis

(Found Only in Men)

What is it?

As has been noted, the prostate gland (which exists only in males) can become inflamed as a result of bacterial or viral invasion. Organisms may enter through the urethra, as do the gonococcus and escherichia coli bacteria, or from other parts of the body. The gland may also become inflamed as a result of an abrupt change in frequency of sexual activity. This condition is called congestive prostatitis.

How could frequency of activity cause inflammation? During periods of sexual arousal, the prostate secretes substances that become part of the semen. It also, like many other glands in the body, develops patterns of response based on the frequency with which it is routinely stimulated, and it manufactures its secretions in anticipation that the pattern will be continued. Thus, if a man establishes a routine of masturbation (or other orgasm-producing activity) three times a day, then abruptly cuts back to no sexual activity, the prostate is caught unprepared — rather like a merchant who has built inventories in anticipation of brisk business only to find that customers suddenly have stopped buying. Secretions accumulate in the gland, congest it, and attract bacteria or viruses that normally would be routinely expelled. The result is inflammation.

Significantly, it is not only suspension of regular activity that brings about the condition; if a man goes abruptly from a schedule of zero orgasmic experiences to several daily — as, for example, in the excitement of meeting a new partner — the prostate may strain to meet the new demands and become congested and inflamed.

Under either of these conditions, prostatitis is not literally a sexually transmitted disease, for no infectious agent passed from one partner to the other. However, it is a sexually precipitated disease — one that can occur homosexually or heterosexually.

How do you know you have it?

The first symptom of prostatitis (whether congestive or another variety) is pain in the pelvic area. It may be felt principally or solely in the rectum, the loin, the testicles, the urethra, or the lower back; or it may be felt in any combination of these areas. It may be felt only on urination or defecation, or it may be felt independently of these activities.

How is it diagnosed?

Tactile examination of the prostate (via insertion of a gloved finger into the rectum) will reveal considerable swelling and tenderness. The feel is usually characterized as "boggy."

Pressure on the prostate should cause material from the infection to be expressed through the urethra. Laboratory analysis of this material will often lead to identification of the infectious organisms. Absence of organisms like the gonococcus or escherichia coli encourages the hypothesis of congestive prostatitis. The patient's history confirms the diagnosis.

How is it treated?

Unlike bacterial prostatitis, the congestive version of the disease does not respond to antibiotics. The usual initial treatment is prostatic massage, that is, the physician inserts a gloved finger into the rectum and presses rhythmically against the prostate gland, causing debris and pus to ooze out through the urethra. It's hoped congestion will not recur. If it does, the massage is repeated. Concurrently, the therapist normally will employ a combination of other treatments, hoping that they will ease the problem and enhance the body's normal recovery mechanism.

Many therapies have developed empirical support over the years. The principal ones and their intended effects are found in Table 1.

How can you avoid it?

A great many men may alter their frequency of sexual activity quite dramatically without suffering congestive prostatitis. The prospects of inflammation are really not likely enough to warrant preventive measures, such as prophylactic masturbation to maintain continuity of prostatic discharge after the abrupt termination of a period of intense activity with a partner.

The simplest advice is to be aware of the possibility of congestive prostatitis following an abrupt change in sexual activity. If symptoms develop, recognize that they may be a result of change in activity, and be sure to inform a physician that this change has taken place.

TABLE 1.
Therapies for Prostatitis

THERAPY	INTENDED EFFECT
Hot baths	Relieve congestion, obtain temporary relief of symptoms.
Avoid spicy foods and alcoholic beverages	Avoid complicating the problem by irritating the inflamed prostate when the patient urinates.
Avoid marijuana	Probably — though not certainly — has the same effect as avoiding spicy foods and alcoholic beverages.

THERAPY	INTENDED EFFECT
Bed rest	General improvement of health, strengthening body to fight infection.
Protect perineum against cold	Insure regular blood flow to prostate and create body atmosphere conducive to healing.
Antihistamine drugs	Eliminate possibility that infection relates to an allergy.
Urethral dilation	Open passage if stricture is involved; open mouth of infected glands.
Smallpox vaccination	If cause is viral, try to obtain any cross-protection possible.
Antitrichomonas drugs	If infection is caused by trichomonas bacterium (possible though unlikely), this will cure it.
Tranquilizers	Remove any aspects of emotional influence.

CHAPTER 15

Venereal Warts

(Transmitted Homosexually among Men and Women)

What are they?

Their medical name is condylomata acuminata (singular: condyloma acuminatum). They are a variety of surface growths believed to be caused by viruses of the papova group. They are "benign" (that is, noncancerous) and can take many forms: they can be as small as the head of a pin or can grow to the size of a dime; they generally have the puffy appearance of a cauliflower, but they may assume a variety of other textures and configurations. They are pink and soft to the touch; they bleed easily, and if rubbed their outer edges may disintegrate into a sort of powder.

They are found on the penis, in the urethra or vagina, and around the anus or mouth. They often appear in only one of these sites, but they may appear in two or more. They are capable of autoinoculation. This means that the virus spreads by contact with the adjacent uninfected portion of flesh. If you ignore them, not only will they not go away, they'll continue to grow until they cover an extensive area. However, it is extremely unlikely that anyone would fail to seek treatment after a short time, for the warts are extremely itchy, and when scratched, they can become painful.

When they occur on the penis, they are usually small and appear in clusters. If they occur under the foreskin (the fold of skin covering the glans of an uncircumcised man), they can fill the entire surface between the corona (the ring of darkened tissue surrounding the glans) and the lowermost fold of the foreskin. Moisture encourages their spread. When in the urethra, they can spread inward toward the prostate and urinary bladder. This can lead to difficult or painful urination or urethral bleeding. When on the anus, they can spread into the rectum as well as out onto the surfaces of the buttocks or along the cleft. It is in the anal area that some of the larger specimens appear. When they invade the rectum, bleeding may occur and defecation may be difficult or painful.

Visually they are identical to condylomata lata, warts that sometimes appear with syphilis. The latter, however, are caused by the syphilis spirochete, whereas the former are caused by a virus.

How do you get them?

For many years, the popular thinking was that condylomata acuminata could be spread only through sexual contact. It is clear now, however, that this is not so. The disease has successfully been reproduced by inoculation of bacteria-free filtrates from the warts into dogs, horses, calves, and human volunteers. The warts also have appeared in members of the same household who report that they had no sexual contact and in physicians who treated the disease. Thus, the virus apparently can be spread by mere touching and possibly also on clothing. Factors that appear to enhance contagion are a long foreskin, warmth in the anogenital region (for example, as a result of tight garments), friction, buildup of fecal matter or other detritus, and perspiration.

Sexual contact with an infected person may, but need not necessarily, transmit the disease. Researchers estimate that the probability of developing condylomata acuminata after sex with an infected person is about 60 to 70 percent. The incubation period — that is, the period before symptoms develop — may be anywhere from one to eight months. The eight-month incubation period was demonstrated when researchers experimentally inoculated the virus into human volunteers and obtained typical warts at the site of the inoculation.

Most people with condylomata acuminata can trace the origin

to a sexual source. Rectal-penile congress is often regarded as the primary means of contagion, but the warts have appeared in the anal region of patients who insist that they had no anal contact. Quite probably the virus reaches the anus by another route. The warts can also develop in the mouth following fellatio. In one case, two men were sexually involved for over a year and generally practiced mutual fellatio. One partner had condylomata on the penis. The other partner developed a wart on the undersurface of his tongue — about one year after the first contact with this partner. The warts were removed from both partners. In a pathology comparison of tissue section, the growths proved virtually identical.

How is the disease diagnosed?

The appearance of condylomata (whether of the acuminatum variety, not associated with syphilis, or the latum variety, associated with that disease) is visually quite distinct from that of nonvenereal warts. If the warts are very large or have been in place for several months, many diagnosticians will want to perform a biopsy to make sure that cancer has not developed. There have been cases where these growths became malignant. Fortunately, prompt treatment usually eliminates this prospect.

How are condylomata acuminata treated?

If the warts are small, they can usually be removed rather easily by applying podophyllin, a dark resin obtained from the mandrake plant, to the surface of each wart. The wart should first be wiped clean, then a small quantity of a solution of podophyllin painted onto the surface with a cotton swab. The chemical will burn away the tissue of the wart. Unfortunately, it will also burn other tissue with which it comes into contact; thus, the physician must be careful not to permit any of it to drip onto surrounding areas of flesh.

Podophyllin treatment can be quite painful. There is usually both itching and surface pain, which can be relieved some-what — but not entirely — by soaking the affected area in water. Often repeated applications of podophyllin are needed, either because the chemical did not completely destroy the warts or because there has been further spread of them. The necessity of washing away the solution before unaffected flesh can be dam-aged makes the treatment less than fully reliable.

Another approach is electrocoagulation (or burning away) of the warts with what is called an "electric needle." This has the advantage of better control of the degree of destruction. How-ever, anesthesia — local for small lesions, general for large ones — is necessary.

A great many other treatments have been attempted, usually without significant success. In one experimental treatment, a vaccine is made from the warts and reinjected into the patient with the hope that the patient's body will develop an immunity to the growths. Some researchers claim to have seen improve-ment; others report no improvement. Additional research with this treatment is in progress.

In another experiment, x-radiation was attempted, as in treat-ment of cancer. The theory was that, like cancer cells, those of the condylomata would be more sensitive to x-radiation than normal cells, because the former are rapidly reproducing and therefore more vulnerable than mature cells. The theory was exciting, but the condylomata kept right on growing. Since radi-ation itself is dangerous — it causes scar tissue and is believed also capable of causing or encouraging certain cancers — the approach was abandoned.

One study was based on the hypothesis that the warts were a reaction to emotional stress. The theory was that psychotherapy and/or hypnotherapy, by overcoming such stress, would heal the warts. The initial study did produce considerable improvement in several sufferers of condylomata, but later researchers were not able to duplicate the initial investigator's reported results.

Interestingly, quite often the warts disappear spontaneously — which must have been the case in the initial psychotherapy-hypnotherapy experiment. In various medical studies, spon-taneous disappearance has occurred in anywhere from 10 percent to 75 percent of all subjects. One patient in whom the warts disappeared under interestingly unusual circumstances was homosexually active and developed a great many warts around his mouth. He grew a mustache and beard to cover them. Various treatments, including podophyllin, were ineffective. The man then developed viral hepatitis. He was bedridden for a month. When he recovered, he shaved the mustache and beard, and the skin surface beneath was completely clear.

A number of patients who underwent electrosurgical removal under anesthesia did not develop recurrences, despite repeated contact with infected partners. Possibly the destruction of the warts electrosurgically brought about an antibody reaction within the patient that prevented reinfection.

When the warts develop deep inside the urethra, treatment is most difficult. The area is not accessible to podophyllin swabs. Electrocautery can produce scar tissue that may obstruct the urethra. Recently various chemical agents have been tried experimentally. The most promising seems to be the drug thiotepa, which is instilled into the urethra weekly. The treatment clearly is preferable to alternative therapies, but it presently remains experimental; long-term effects are not known.

When the condylomata are on or under the foreskin, circumcision is a useful procedure. It not only removes some of the warts themselves but also eliminates the moist area that tends to encourage additional development of condylomata.

These growths are particularly problematic when they are in the vagina of a pregnant woman. They may interfere with passage of the baby and possibly may be contracted by the baby. Some specialists believe it is dangerous to treat pregnant women for genital warts because the chemical or surgical procedures can disturb the fetus. They suggest cesarean section to avoid infecting the baby.

CHAPTER 16

Herpes Infections

(*Transmitted Homosexually among Men and Women*)

What is herpes?

Herpes is a family of viruses. There are two principal types, unimaginatively named Type I and Type II. The former attacks the mouth, lips, throat, eyes, stomach, skin of the face, neck and upper torso, and in rare cases the brain. The latter attacks the lower torso and legs of adults, particularly the anogenital region, but also can infect the newborn, causing nerve damage and possibly death within several days.

Fearsome though the effects are on babies, the adult version of the disease is relatively innocuous. Indeed, herpes Type I is, when it develops on the lips and face, nothing more than the very familiar "cold sore."

How do you get it?

It is not clear how either of these viruses is transmitted. Presumably contact is involved, and presumably that contact is usually sexual — at least in the broadest sense (kissing and caressing as well as genital and/or anorectal contact). However, there are cases of herpes in which a person's only sexual partner has no evidence of herpetic infection. Probably there is a carrier state — though, if this is so, it still does not explain how the virus is transmitted from one body to the other.

How do you know you have herpes?

The first symptom is one or more (usually at least three) small and painful bumps or blisters. In Type I infections, the most common site is the mouth, lips, or adjacent surfaces of the face.

In Type II infections (also called herpes progenitalis), the most common site is the genitals and the next most common the anus. In men with genital symptoms, the lesions usually appear on the glans or shaft of the penis; they are much less frequently found on the scrotum or in the groin. In women with genital symptoms, the genital lips (inner or outer) are the most common site; sores develop much less frequently on the clitoris or inside the vagina, although cervical lesions may develop.

Whatever the site, the bumps (or blisters) generally grow increasingly tender for about forty-eight hours, much in the same way that a pimple or boil comes to a head. Then they rupture to form soft, extremely painful open sores on a reddish base. Within about five days, the sores become less painful and begin to heal. The skin is replaced gradually, working its way inward from the edges of each sore. Usually, within ten to twenty days healing is complete with little if any scarring.

Note that this all takes place without treatment of any kind. However, in many cases, the sores will reappear in the future. The when and why of reappearance are unclear, but in many cases reappearance correlates with emotional strain or a general rundown condition, brought on by fever, cold, fatigue, or even sunburn. Presumably the virus has not left the body but merely become dormant after being attacked by the body's natural defense mechanisms; when the body is weakened, the ability to maintain defenses is lessened and the infection reappears. In some cases, an initial or recurrent infection is complicated by development of a superimposed bacterial infection that causes increased ulceration, pain, and swelling, and delays healing.

Some venereologists believe that herpes is the most common cause of genital ulceration. In any case, when multiple sores appear on the genitals, herpes should be suspected.

How is herpes diagnosed?

One simple test to distinguish herpes from syphilis, chancroid, or other diseases producing similar lesions is for a physician to scrape the suspicious lesion, collect the resultant detritus, place it on a slide, and stain it by the Papanicolau method. This involves applying a chemical coloring to the smear that allows the observer to study the internal structure of the cells under a microscope. If one of the herpes viruses is present, the cells will have a characteristic appearance.

Further studies can be done using tissue cultures. The virus can be incubated on special cells and then studied for certain identification. Other laboratory tests of blood serum can reveal a herpes antibody; however, these tests are less than foolproof and are not readily available.

How is the disease treated?

As has been noted, herpes infection will go away without treatment, though it may recur. No known agent will kill the virus. There are treatments that attempt to quicken the natural course of the disease; however, while some of these offer symptomatic relief, they are of no demonstrated value in preventing recurrence. Probably the most a victim can do is keep the area clean, apply a topical anesthetic ointment if the pain is severe, and avoid sex until the lesions have healed. Sexual relations will not exacerbate the disease, but there is the possibility of infecting a partner.

How can you avoid herpes?

Not knowing how the disease is spread, we are hard put to advise about avoiding it. Logically, it is a good idea not to have sexual relations with a person who has symptoms. We advise not only avoiding contact with the symptomatic part of the body but avoiding sexual relations completely. In other words, if the person has an infection on the mouth or anus, don't feel that you will be safe by avoiding these areas and having genital contact. When the infection is in the body, it may spread (though we are by no means certain that it will) through contact with surfaces other than those displaying symptoms.

A few additional points about herpes infections:

Many researchers suspect that herpes Type II is in some way

involved in cancer of the cervix in females. Oncologist Laure Aurelian, at Johns Hopkins Medical Center in Baltimore, has demonstrated a correlation between Type II and cervical cancer; she has identified the same viral pattern in cervical tumor cells and has shown that cells taken from cervical cancers contain herpes Type II materials. Dr. Aurelian has also demonstrated that 90 percent of patients with cervical cancers have antibodies to herpes Type II.

The question arises as to whether introduction of the herpes virus into the rectum during anal intercourse might not be a cause for cancer in the male. There is not at present any persuasive evidence of this, but the possibility certainly cannot be overlooked. Considering the many similarities between the atmospheres of the rectum and the vagina (warmth, moisture, etc.), the potential for a similar carcinogenic action would seem to exist.

If herpes Type II is not itself carcinogenic (cancer producing), there may be a link through a method of treatment called phototherapy, in which a light-sensitive dye is applied to the viral lesion and then light administered to the lesion. Some investigators believe that this treatment changes the herpes virus in some way, giving it a carcinogenic potential that it otherwise would not possess.

A third herpes virus, named cytomegalovirus, has recently come under suspicion as another sexually transmitted disease. Its usual symptoms are fever, swollen glands, and sore throat in adults, and signs of nervous system damage in babies. The mode of transmission is unknown but may be sexual. The organism is quite common, probably being found in 80 percent of persons over age thirty-five, but the incidence of disease states among these people is unknown.

The disease apparently is not harmful to adults, but intrauterine infection of the fetus is believed to be a major cause of mental retardation and other abnormalities in children. The seriousness of infection acquired at birth is undetermined; however, babies infected at birth appear to develop less severe problems than those infected during pregnancy. Infection in infants is presently estimated at about 1 percent of all live births in the United States.

CHAPTER 17

Molluscum Contagiosum

(Transmitted Homosexually among Men
and Women)

What is it?

It is a contagious disease of the skin that is worldwide in distribution and encountered most frequently in children and young adults. The primary symptom is a series of small, smooth papules each having a slight depression in the center. They occur on the face, lips, arms, legs, buttocks, genitals, scalp, eyelids, and in rare instances on the mucous membranes of the mouth. Contrary to the similar symptoms of other sexually transmitted diseases, these lesions never appear on the soles or palms. The infectious agent is a virus belonging to the pox virus family.

How do you get it?

Molluscum contagiosum is spread by close physical contact with an infected person. This contact need not be sexual, but sexual contact is one of the most likely ways of bringing the infected surfaces of one person's skin into contact with the surfaces of another person's skin.

How is it diagnosed?

The symptoms may appear anywhere from fourteen to fifty days after contact. The characteristic papules do not resemble the lesions of other diseases. Thus, preliminary diagnosis may be made on sight and confirmed by microscopic examination of a slide containing a specimen from the papule.

How is it treated?

The treatment of choice is removal of all lesions by curettage (scraping) or electrodissection. If not removed, the lesions may spread through autoinoculation.

How can the disease be avoided?

It appears that there are no asymptomatic carriers of molluscum contagiosum. Thus, if you avoid contact with people who have the lesions, you should avoid contracting the disease. Fortunately, while the lesions are uncomfortable and in some cases unsightly, there is no evidence that the disease is dangerous.

CHAPTER 18

Lice and Mites

(Transmitted Homosexually among Men and Women)

Here are two you *can* catch from a toilet seat. More frequently, however, they are transmitted by sexual contact.

What are they?

They are identical except for the infesting organism, which in one case is a louse (a full-grown insect) and in the other a mite (a microscopic organism).

The louse is the *Phthirus pubis,* and as the second word in that Latin name suggests, the favored nesting ground is the pubis — more specifically, the pubic hair. This "pubic louse" also is called a "crab louse" because under a microscope it looks very much like a crab, with pairs of claws and four pairs of tiny legs. Without a microscope, it looks like a brown dot approximately the size of a pinhead. Its appearance under a microscope gives rise to its vernacular name, "the crabs."

The mite has the Latin name of *Sarcoptes scabiei hominis,* which usually is abbreviated to "scabies." It is too small to be seen with the naked eye, and its chief symptom is intense itchiness; thus, it sometimes is known simply as "the itch."

How do you get them?

Either of these parasites can be transmitted by close personal contact, not necessarily sexual, or on bedding, clothing, or other personal items. Scabies can also be transmitted by dogs, cats, or other animals.

If separated from a human host for twenty-four hours, both parasites will die. They can, however, switch from host to host during that period, and thus you can get them from a toilet seat.

How do you know you have them? ─────────────

Pubic lice produce intense itching in some people but no itching in others. The itchiness, it has been theorized, is an allergic reaction to the bites of the louse as it sucks blood from its human host, but not all hosts develop the allergy. If you do not itch, you may carry the lice indefinitely without realizing you are infested, for these parasites are virtually unnoticeable in the pubic hair, especially against the skin of Caucasians and Orientals; against black skin, the yellowish-gray color of the louse's body is more apparent.

Scratching the infested area does not generally relieve itching and may carry the pubic lice on the fingers to other hairy parts of the body, including the head, armpits, and the male chest and thighs. In some people, the bites of the lice cause a mild rash composed of small, sky-blue spots.

The life span of the pubic louse is thirty days, so if you should happen to be infested by just one gender of them, your problem should eventually prove self-solving. Much more often, however, you will be infested by at least one male and one female. The female lays about three eggs a day, which hatch in seven to nine days. Thus, within three weeks after the infesting contact, the average person has a veritable colony of lice.

The initial infestation of scabies will usually produce no symptoms. Itching will begin after a month and become progressively intense. As a result of scratching, the infested areas of the skin then develop small groups of open sores. Most sufferers report that the itching is worse at night.

The scabies mite favors warm, moist areas of the body — especially the groin, folds in the genital flesh, inner surfaces of the thighs, the wrists, and the areas between the fingers. The mites are small enough to burrow through the skin and reside just beneath the surface. Thus, while you scratch at them, they happily burrow along, completely invulnerable to your assault.

How is diagnosis made?

Positive diagnosis of pubic lice is made by finding a louse or its eggs — an easy enough matter if one looks closely. Diagnosis of scabies is somewhat more difficult. The history, location, and appearance of the skin sores strongly suggest infestation, especially if people with whom you have had contact are also itching. However, to confirm the diagnosis, scrapings of the sores must be examined under a microscope for presence of the mite. Often the mite is impossible to capture, making confirmation impossible.

How are these infestations treated?

Treatment of choice for both is local application of gamma benzene hexachloride, which is marketed in cream, lotion, or shampoo form under the brand name Kwell.

With lice, massage the cream or lotion into the affected area and leave it there for twenty-four hours without washing. Then wash thoroughly. If you use the shampoo — which is generally less effective except in infestation of the scalp — work it into a lather for about five minutes, then rinse out immediately. Be careful not to get it into the vagina or the urethral meatus, for it may cause irritation. If itching does not vanish after twenty-four hours, repeat the treatment — but never more than twice within one week.

In cases of scabies, apply either the cream, lotion, or shampoo to the entire body surface below the neck after a hot soapy shower. Do not rinse for twenty-four hours. If itching persists after forty-eight hours, repeat the treatment — but not more than twice within one week.

Other medications are available, but they generally are not as effective as gamma benzene hexachloride. This preparation can be purchased without a prescription.

How can these infestations be avoided?

It often takes a week or longer for lice or mites to develop to such an extent that the host realizes he or she is infested. People with whom there is contact during this period can acquire the parasites without either party realizing what is happening. Thus, a monogamous relationship is the only foolproof way of avoiding infestation. However, inspection of a prospective partner's skin may provide evidence of scratching indicative of scabies or some other disorder, and truly sharp-eyed may even observe one or more pubic lice. Obviously, if you believe a prospective partner may be infested, the prudent thing is to ask about it before having contact. In some cases a person may enter a sexual liaison knowing that he or she is infected.

CHAPTER 19

Sexual Injury

Almost all sexual injury occurs anorectally among males, and, more specifically, is suffered by the person who is penetrated rather than the person doing the penetrating. Why should anorectal penetration be more apt to cause injury than penetration of the vagina? A comparison of the anus/rectum and vagina provides the answer (see Table 2).

The vagina, it will be noted, has muscles through its entire length. They are capable of expanding as the penis enters. The muscles at the entrance are not particularly tight. Indeed, they are capable of expanding to the size of a baby's head.

There are no muscles in the rectum itself. The only muscles in the anorectal system are in the anal sphincter. They are extremely versatile — indeed, they are the only muscles in the body capable of differentiating among solids, liquids, and gas, and expanding or contracting to accommodate the passage of each. But their capacity to stretch is limited. If they exceed that capacity, they will rupture or permanently stretch. The result is fecal incontinence, i.e., inability to retain feces.

Of course, the vaginal muscles may also stretch or tear — and sometimes do, especially in childbirth. But the vagina is capable of accommodating much larger circumferences than the anus. In any case, while rupture or stretching of the vaginal muscles may render the organ less pleasing for the woman or her partner, there is no interference with excretion or other bodily functions.

Another important difference between the two organs: the vagina secretes lubricants that facilitate penetration, at least until menopause, but there are no natural lubricants in the anus/rectum. If adequate amounts of synthetic lubricants, such as

Vaseline or K-Y Jelly, are not used, penetration may injure the anus or lead to development of abscesses.

The vaginal walls are thick and solid; they are anchored in place by surrounding body tissue. The rectum is a narrow tube held in place only by the tissues at its ends, connecting it to the anus and colon. Thus, its walls are susceptible to herniation.

The veins in the vaginal wall are all supported by muscle. The veins in the rectum — by name, the hemorrhoidal veins — have no support. Trouble frequently arises even if rectal penetration does not take place (the well-known problem called hemorrhoids), but this condition is much more likely to occur — and in a much more serious form — when there has been penetration.

The vagina is in close proximity to the urethra and bladder. This can lead to episodes of cystitis or urethritis. These problems do not normally attend rectal penetration, but a similar problem exists with the prostate: it can become inflamed as a result of pressure from the penis, a finger, or some other object used for penetration.

Let us consider some of these problems in greater detail:

Hemorrhoids

The veins in the wall of the rectum normally lie flat. They are shielded from the rectal passageway only by a very thin layer of tissue. At times and for reasons that researchers do not fully understand, these veins become stretched and dilated. They then bulge out into the rectal passageway. You can appreciate what they look like if you have ever seen someone with very severe varicose veins of the legs. The hemorrhoidal veins develop that same swollen, stretched, twisted, dilated, "full" appearance.

As feces pass through the rectum, they rub against the thin walls of the swollen veins. If stools are firm, abrasions are created and bleeding occurs. Of course, any firm object can cause abrasions — a finger, a penis, a vibrator.

Anal penetration brings on or aggravates hemorrhoids in two

TABLE 2.

Comparison of anus/rectum and vagina in terms of problems attending penile penetration

VAGINA	Problem	RECTUM	Problem
Opening Wide at surface, expands readily		Anus narrow with no expansion possible	Fissures, tears
Walls Firmly held to body		Not firmly held to body	Parts of wall herniate out through the anus
Muscles Entire vagina		Only at sphincter	Muscle stretches, fecal incontinence develops
Veins No nonsupported veins in wall		Hemorrhoidal veins in wall — no support over the veins	Hemorrhoidal problem
Lubricant Naturally occurring	Decreases after menopause	No natural lubricant	Lubricant (Vaseline, etc.,) must be supplied

VAGINA (cont.)	Problem (cont.)	RECTUM (cont.)	Problem (cont.)
Lubricant (cont.)			Trauma to walls of anus, fissures, perianal abscesses
Bacteria Normal bacteria nonpathogenic for male urethra	Occasionally can develop and transmit trichomoniasis infection nonsexually	Many normal bacteria that are pathogenic for urethra	Urethritis, prostatitis
Nonsexual diseases Possibly tuberculosis, B-group of streptococci, urinary tract infections	Urethral transmission	Many intestinal diseases, possibly tuberculosis	Hepatitis A, amebiasis, shigellosis

principal ways. First, the thrusting of the penis against the rectal walls tends to bring the veins to the surface. Second, the attempt to tighten the anus to grasp the penis changes the blood pressure in the area and causes an increased "back" pressure (or return pressure) against the inner walls of the veins, causing bulging and stretching. The result of this is a marked distension of the veins. Almost unbelievably large protruding hemorrhoids have been found in people who play the receptor during anal intercourse.

Can hemorrhoids be avoided? Probably not, even if you do not perform anal penetration, but their effects can be minimized. The condition can be alleviated somewhat if one avoids straining while defecating. To avoid strain, adjust your diet to include more bulk-type foods that present a large amount of undigested roughage. This acts as a mechanical stimulant that aids evacuation. Foods include cereals (especially bran), vegetables, fruits, and nuts. Studies indicate that prune juice helps increase stool weight and water content, which further encourages evacuation; it also contains a natural laxative. Synthetic laxatives available in pharmacies also aid evacuation, but they can create more problems than they solve; we do not recommend them — although we do favor compounds containing psyllium hydrophilic mucilloid, which increase stool weight without laxative action. Rectal suppositories can also assist in avoiding strain during defecation, at the same time easing pain and itchiness of hemorrhoids.

Among people who serve as receptors anally, hemorrhoids may be aggravated additionally by enemas, taken to empty the rectum and thus facilitate penile intromission. Still another problem involves the synthetic lubricant generally used to facilitate penetration. As thrusting continues, the lubricant wears thin. If additional quantities are not applied regularly throughout the act, the penis may further traumatize the hemorrhoids.

Thus, to minimize damage and suffering of hemorrhoids: (1) observe a diet with considerable roughage (bulk-type foods), (2) drink 4 to 6 ounces of prune juice daily, (3) if needed, use a stool softener (e.g., dioctyl sodium sulfosuccinate), (4) apply lubricant regularly and repeatedly during penetration.

Anal Fissures

A fissure is a linear tear. In the anorectal area such tears usually lie along the rectal midline, extending downward into the anus. This can cause spasm of the anal sphincter, a very painful condition. Indeed, many sufferers try to avoid moving their bowels because the pain is so intense. This self-induced constipation causes further difficulties, for stools become hard and large, and then, when defecation does occur, it is even more painful and tends to increase the size of the fissure.

To minimize damage, dilate the anus gently and gradually before attempting penetration. Begin with one finger, using plenty of lubrication. Massage the anus, relaxing and stretching the muscle, until one finger can pass quite easily. Then proceed to a second finger, achieving this same ease of penetration, before attempting penile entry. Again — remember to apply lubrication profusely at every stage of the act.

The usual treatment for anal fissures is rest. That is, the patient is advised to avoid anorectal penetration and straining bowel movements. Diet and other techniques described in the section on hemorrhoids are employed to soften stools. It is hoped the fissure will heal on its own. If not, corrective surgery may be undertaken; however, it is complicated and painful, and success is by no means assured.

Anal Sphincter Exhaustion or Decompensation

Repeated dilatation of the anal sphincter will eventually cause the normal tonic state of the sphincter to weaken or give way to a state of physiologic exhaustion or decompensation. Two things happen: the ring of muscles at the anus loses its mechanical ability to contract, and the muscles stretch; their increased length makes it impossible for them to draw together to form a tight closure. The result is that the person can no longer retain feces.

There are several surgical treatments, none wholly satisfactory. Probably the most common is the Thiersch operation, which involves insertion of a string through the anal muscular ring to tighten it. Obviously, this is at its very best a poor substitute for nature.

Damage from Foreign Objects

It is particularly dangerous to insert a foreign object into the rectum. People often fail to appreciate the danger; they believe that they can control the depth of penetration and remove the object at will. This is not always so.

The anal sphincter and the walls of the rectum have a certain degree of muscle tone; that is, they always possess a certain level of contraction or "tightness." (This is true of many passageways, including the throat and numerous organs inside the abdomen.)

When a foreign body enters the area, it pushes against the surfaces of the organ. In reply, the surfaces undergo contraction — a "grasping" or "drawing in" action. A foreign body inserted into the rectum can be literally pulled in beyond a point where it is easily retrievable.

Since foreign materials often are used for anorectal stimulation, the number of them lost inside the rectum is considerable. Most are small, but physicians have removed such large items as a six-ounce Coca-Cola bottle, an entire pencil, and a vibrator head. *Modern Medicine,* a magazine for physicians, recently reported the intrarectal loss (and subsequent retrieval, via forceps) of an after-shaving lotion bottle that measured 21.5 centimeters in circumference and 14.2 in length — comparable in size to a wine bottle.

The degree of damage caused by the insertion of any item depends on its size, the force applied, and the amount of lubrication. The larger the object, the greater the force, and the less the lubrication, the more severe the damage is likely to be. Injury can range from a simple contusion, or bruise, to an actual tear in the wall. When the latter occurs, fecal matter may spill into the abdominal cavity, creating infection that may prove fatal.

Even if a lost object does not damage the wall immediately, it represents a danger, for the bowel cannot be evacuated — at least not as readily — and there is the likelihood of trauma to the rectal wall as evacuation is attempted.

Removal of a foreign body may prove extremely difficult even under the best medical circumstances. Sometimes damage to the rectum will occur as the item is being removed. If the rectal wall is torn, surgery generally will be necessary, along with treatment of any infection that may develop.

Damage from Penile Insertion

Like foreign objects, the penis itself can damage the rectal wall if it is inserted violently or at an unusual angle. If the penis hits the wall directly — that is, if it is inserted at an angle perpendicular to the rectal wall — the direct application of force to the wall could cause substantial injury.

As with foreign objects, if the rectal wall is torn, surgery generally will be necessary, along with treatment of any infection.

Proctitis

Proctitis is an inflammation of the rectal mucosa, characterized by pain, a constant urge to defecate, diarrhea, tenesmus (a painful spasm with involuntary straining), and bleeding. The area of inflammation can develop multiple small ulcers and even multiple abscesses (pockets of flesh filled with pus).

There are a number of causes of proctitis that have nothing to do with anal intercourse, but it is easy to see why penetration can produce this inflammation: the act involves multiple traumatic insults to the wall of the rectum by penile intrusion, combined with introduction of foreign bacteria on the penis. It is also possible that repeated penile intrusions will cause minute breaks in the rectal mucosal wall, with the result that bacteria of the rectum invade the wall.

When proctitis develops, rectal penetration should be discontinued. However, few sufferers need to be told this, for the pain is so severe and the area so irritated and tender that many patients can scarcely bear even the entry of an examiner's lubricated gloved finger.

Diagnosis of proctitis is difficult. A determination must be made as to whether the condition is an infection (for example, gonorrhea, amebiasis, tuberculosis) or the effects of drugs that irritate the intestine, such as antibiotics. In the absence of other positive findings, if there is a history of frequent rectal penetration, a good preliminary diagnosis is that the condition was brought on traumatically.

Treatment generally comprises warm sitz baths — that is, sitting in a tub of hot water, which provides much relief to the area as well as helping to combat infection — stool softeners or antidiarrheal drugs, and pain killers.

Proctitis is usually not a dangerous condition, but it is uncomfortable in the extreme.

Irritative Prostatitis

The prostate gland is located against the rectal wall, less than a finger's length into the rectum. Frequently during anal penetration, the penis will apply pressure directly against the gland or will move the rectal wall in such a way that pressure is felt. The prostate apparently connects to numerous erogenously sensitive nerve endings, for many people find this pressure quite stimulating.

Unfortunately, repeated trauma of the prostate by the penis (or a finger or other stimulus) causes inflammation, which usually leads to swelling, pain, and tenderness.

Diagnosis of prostatitis is, as we noted in a previous chapter, quite difficult. A number of diseases may cause this inflammation, as may such apparently innocuous factors as an abrupt change in frequency of orgasm (congestive prostatitis). When none of these factors seems to be operative and there is a history of anal activity, irritative prostatitis is likely.

Treatment consists of hot sitz baths and cessation of sexual activity until the condition is healed.

Perianal and Rectal Abscesses —————————————

An abscess is a circumscribed collection of pus, that is, a pocket of flesh filled with pus. It may occur in just about any part of the body and is caused by infection.

Among people who frequently experience anorectal penetration, abscesses of the anus, perineum, or rectum are far more common than in the general population. Apparently they develop from minute tears or abrasions that are promptly invaded by foreign bacteria. They are usually very painful.

Diagnosis is by inspection: an abscess has a distinct appearance. Treatment is with hot sitz baths, which provide relief and combat inflammation; antibiotics, chosen on a basis of cultures; and sometimes bed rest and analgesics (painkillers). If an abscess is particularly large, unusually located, or unresponsive to other therapies, it may have to be opened surgically and drained.

As can be seen, the possibilities for injury during anal stimulation are considerable. Some specialists believe that such injury is inevitable and that penetration should therefore be avoided at all costs. Others feel that prospects of serious injury are sufficiently remote to make this sweeping proscription unnecessary when both partners are careful. But clearly, the less frequently one experiences anal invasion, the less likely one is to incur such injury.

The Medical Facts about Enemas—————————————

Many people employ enemas in conjunction with sexual activity. The usual reason is to clear the bowel to facilitate penile intromission. However, some people find the enema itself arousing, and others are aroused by giving an enema.

Are enemas safe? If so, what liquid should be used? What substances may safely be added to the liquid?

Enemas are relatively safe. Medically speaking, any interference with the body's natural functioning is undesirable, and enemas are indeed such an interference. They wash away intestinal organisms which are helpful in digestion. Performed with any frequency, they can create a dependency by reducing the body's reliance on natural evacuation mechanisms. Still, enemas do not represent an interference as great as, say, anal intercourse. The frequency with which they are performed is the key to their safety or danger. Few proctologists would consider one a year excessive. Almost all proctologists would consider one a day excessive. So where to draw the line? One a week? One a month?

Probably one a week can be tolerated without serious problem. We stress, however, that in the opinion of most trained observers, the fewer enemas you take, the better.

What liquid should be used? The safest is simple lukewarm water. The usual amount is slightly more than two quarts. When a slight irritative effect is needed to help produce a bowel movement, use about one and three-quarter quarts of water with five ounces of mild soap suds.

Some people use whiskey, wine, or beer in an enema to produce a feeling of intoxication. There is little question that the intestines can absorb enough alcohol to bring on the desired effect, but alcohol can be quite irritating to the tender tissues of the rectum and large intestine.

Some devotees of enemas ask about "high colonics," which occasionally are administered at naturopath-type health spas. These enemas involve spraying large quantities of water into the upper reaches of the rectum — specifically, the area of the colon. Devotees believe there is health advantage to this.

We are convinced that there is none. High colonics certainly do not "cleanse" anything. Any materials that they wash away either would be evacuated in due course or are part of the natural environment of the rectum. It seems that the only reason these enemas are given is because some people find it pleasurable to have the rectum and colon suffused with water.

Why is this pleasurable? There are a great many sexually sensitive nerve endings in the region. They are stimulated by pressure — manual, penile, oral, or even the pressure of water. In some cases, no doubt, psychological factors also come into play.

People sometimes ask about "air" enemas for sexual arousal.

The air could be administered with a bicycle pump, orally, or by some other means.

There is no question that some people find this pleasurable. Again, there is pressure on sexually sensitive nerve endings, including those in the prostate region, and there may be psychological delights as well. However, pumping air into the rectum is fraught with danger. The chief risk is that air can pass into the bloodstream and cause damage in other areas of the body, such as the brain or lungs. In some cases, death will result.

It is true that air is used in certain x-ray studies of the intestines, specifically to detect cancer; but this is done under highly controlled circumstances with emergency equipment nearby, and in any case the possible benefits are deemed worth the risk. When the only benefits are recreational, we consider the practice ill-advised.

In sum, enemas can indeed be pleasurable for some people, but even at their most innocuous they pose at least a slight medical threat.

Anorectal Hygiene

Anorectal hygiene is important for medical as well as aesthetic reasons — particularly when the anus and rectum are the focus of sexual activity.

Rectal hygiene starts with good personal hygiene. Keeping the body clean deters infection, fungus disease, and the accumulation of simple debris from the skin. This is particularly important in the anal region. Adequate washing prevents perianal infection and the development of itchy fungus growths.

Daily washing of the anus and the cleft between the buttocks will keep the area relatively free from bacteria and other organisms. Rub soap into the cleft with your hands, or use a washcloth. If anal itch or irritation develops, the best treatment is a hot sitz bath — simply draw several inches of water into a tub and sit in it. This should be done as often as is necessary to provide relief — two or three times daily for fifteen minutes at a time is probably the most popular regimen. Suggested temperature is 100 degrees Fahrenheit.

Afterwards, wipe the area dry with a clean white turkish towel. Vigorous drying will physically dislodge any surface materials that may be causing irritation. Next, apply a simple talcum powder or corn starch; the latter has the advantage of being less likely to cause an allergic reaction. If the condition persists after a week, antifungus drugs or even antibiotics may be called for — especially if your discomfort is great. Physicians who specialize in treating disorders of this sort are called proctologists or colorectal surgeons.

Good bowel habits are immensely helpful in avoiding rectal and anal difficulty. As noted earlier in this chapter, a diet high in bulk encourages regular bowel movements without strain — and without laxatives. Most physicians favor avoiding laxatives entirely. Probably the least undesirable of the various laxatives available are the "bulk" type; they are believed to function by adding bulk materials which require expulsion and thus stimulate the activity of the colon.

Before anal sexual penetration, gentle dilatation is very important. Synthetic lubrication should be applied at the start and regularly throughout the act.

CHAPTER 20

Problems in Sexual Performance

Ultimately, all problems in sexual performance are reducible to one: inability to satisfy oneself and one's partner. This is true whatever the gender of the partner; however, in homosexual activity the problem often manifests itself somewhat differently than in heterosexual activity.

Performance problems among males fall into two categories: impotence and hasty ejaculation. Impotence may take one of several forms: the man may be completely unable to get an erection; or, if he can get one, he may be unable to sustain it until orgasm; or he may be able to do both but only under certain circumstances. In hasty ejaculation, a man might be unable to withhold orgasm even long enough to establish intromission; or if he can do this, he cannot continue the act long enough to satisfy a partner.

Among women, the usual problem is difficulty achieving orgasm: either she cannot do so under any circumstance, or she can only under extraordinary circumstances, or she can but not solely on the basis of the usual stimulation provided by her partner.

Let us consider the problems as they manifest themselves in homosexual relationships.

Female — Orgasmic Difficulties

While a great many women have difficulty achieving orgasm in heterosexual relations — indeed, studies by Kinsey and Masters and Johnson and others reveal that as many as 25 percent of all heterosexually active women have never achieved orgasm during coitus — relatively few have difficulty in homosexual relationships. This probably owes to the following factors:

• The clitoris is the primary source of sexual stimulation in women; it is not stimulated automatically during coitus, and many couples do not know how to position themselves in such a way that it gets stimulated. Meanwhile, homosexually active women often are quite adept at providing clitoral stimulation, and homosexual acts among women generally involve direct clitoral stimulation.

• Even if a man knows how to stimulate the clitoris — manually, orally, coitally, or in other ways — many men seem not terribly interested in providing this stimulation, especially after they have grown comfortable in a relationship. One rarely if ever hears these complaints voiced about homosexual partners.

• Many women are fearful of coitus and may also fear other heterosexual activity. This is especially true among younger unmarried women who come from families in which they have been raised to think of nonmarital sex as wrong. However, the attitudes often carry over into marriage, and in some cases also develop among women whose background is not so rigid. A woman may fear pregnancy or venereal disease. If she met her partner only recently, she may fear that he is exploiting her and/or that he will lose respect for her if she consents. In homosexual relations, fear of pregnancy obviously is not a factor. Usually, neither is fear that a partner is exploiting oneself or will lose respect. Venereal disease is far less common among women whose activity is exclusively homosexual, and most know it.

• Studies by Kinsey and Masters and Johnson and other researchers show a correlation between masturbation and the ability to achieve orgasm in an act with a partner. Masturbation, it seems, trains a woman to seek the kinds of pressures that stimulate orgasm. Practiced over a period of years, it also probably helps overcome feelings of guilt about sex. Women who have overcome the social taboos against homosexual activity are more likely to have also overcome the social taboos against masturbation than women who pursue the exclusively heterosexual, virgin-till-marriage life-style idealized by some.

All this having been said, the fact remains that some women do have problems achieving orgasm in homosexual relations. Some of them may be unable to have an orgasm under any circumstances, while others may succeed during masturbation and/or heterosexual relations. Still others may succeed homosexually but only under certain circumstances, for instance, while intoxicated or while with a certain partner but not with others.

If a woman has never achieved orgasm, there is a slight but real chance that the problem may be entirely physical. This is especially likely if she has a long history of sexual activity. Indeed, the longer she has been active sexually without achieving orgasm, the likelier it is that she has a physical problem.

Psychologist John Money of the Johns Hopkins School of Medicine, in Baltimore, has demonstrated that many women who suffer hormone deficiencies cannot achieve orgasm or can do so only with great effort. In other studies, inability to achieve orgasm has been linked to lesions or adhesions involving the genital organs, especially the clitoris.

Another physical barrier to orgasm in women is neural malfunction: if "messages" received by the sense receptors are not properly transmitted to the brain, orgasm and sometimes even sexual arousal may prove impossible. Dietary inadequacies, leading to certain vitamin shortages or other nutritional lacks, may also inhibit orgasm, as may heavy use of alcohol or other drugs.

As has been noted, physical factors should be investigated if a woman has never had orgasm, especially if she has a long history of sexual activity. They are even more suspect if she once was able to achieve orgasm regularly but no longer can. However, if she is able to achieve orgasm heterosexually but not homosexually, or if she has a long history of unpredictable orgasm (no matter what the gender of a partner), then psychological factors are more probable. Here are some common influences:

HOMOSEXUAL GUILT
The woman believes homosexual relations are morally wrong or for some other reason impermissible. Or she cannot accept the

image of being a "lesbian." She may not admit to these attitudes; she may not even be aware that she possesses them. But they may exist, nonetheless, and their force may be overwhelming. Look for homosexual guilt especially among women who are very secretive about their homosexual activity — women who don't want their families or friends to know, women who make a great effort socially to present themselves as having only heterosexual interests. Consider this possibility also, of course, if a woman achieves orgasm with little or no difficulty heterosexually (in other words, the woman feels guilty about homosexual activity but not heterosexual activity).

FEAR OF FAILURE
Sometimes a woman who has difficulty achieving orgasm will approach each act wondering whether or not she will succeed this time. She may focus so intently on the question that she will distract herself from the stimulation she is receiving. In a sense, she becomes more an observer of the act than a participant. This, naturally, makes her partner's task all the more difficult — and makes orgasm all the less likely to be achieved. If she fails to achieve it, she approaches future acts even more doubtful of her ability. Thus develops a vicious circle in which failure begets self-doubt and self-doubt begets failure. Look for this problem especially among women who suffer feelings of sexual inadequacy or self-doubt. Of course, fear of failure can — and often does — manifest itself in heterosexual as well as homosexual relations.

PERFECTIONISM
This is the other side of the "fear of failure" coin. Some women become so concerned with sexual achievement — with having the best possible orgasm every time, with enjoying sex to the fullest possible degree — that they, too, become distracted from the stimulation they are receiving. If an orgasm is less than a real bell-ringer, they tend to berate themselves and/or their partners. But if orgasm is subpar, it often will be *because* of the woman's perfectionistic distraction. Another vicious circle begins, with orgasms becoming decreasingly satisfying. If an en-

counter ends without orgasm, the woman's perfectionism may give way to fear of failure — and *that* vicious circle may begin. Look for this problem especially among the "sexual athletes," for whom quantity and quality of orgasm are oft-expressed concerns. As with fear of failure, perfectionism can be a problem heterosexually as well as homosexually.

LACK OF INTEREST IN A SPECIFIC PARTNER
In the best of all possible sexual worlds, everyone who found someone else appealing would also be found appealing by that person. In this world, it often does not happen that way. Yet, people sometimes pursue relationships with persons whom they do not find sexually attractive. This may be the case when the person is admired for other qualities: intelligence, achievement, kindness, understanding. Or the person might be seen as a source of financial support. Or in certain circumstances, the person might be one of relatively few partners available; for instance, a girl going to high school in a small town might be attracted to a dozen of her classmates, all of whom practice heterosexual exclusivity, and not attracted to the only two girls in the school who are homosexually active. A series of encounters with partners whom she does not find attractive might lead a woman to conclude that she is incapable of orgasm. This, in turn, could lead to fear of failure in future acts, thus making orgasm even less likely.

INHIBITING SURROUNDINGS
The circumstances under which sex takes place can inhibit orgasm. Physical discomfort (as in an automobile on a cold night) or fear of being discovered can be sufficiently distracting to prevent orgasm.

APPARENTLY IRRELEVANT DISTRACTIONS
Preoccupations of any kind can inhibit orgasm. Fear and anxiety states having nothing whatever to do with sex or with one's present partner (for example, fear of an airplane flight one is scheduled to take tomorrow), family problems, grief (as over the death of a loved one), work-related problems, and a host of other

apparently irrelevant distractions may extinguish sexual desire and/or the ability to achieve orgasm.

Most of the above factors will rarely if ever come into play for most homosexually active women. Indeed, the few studies that contain data about incidence of orgasm in homosexual activity suggest that the vast majority of homosexually active women achieve orgasm regularly and with little or no difficulty. Among those who do not, however, an entire constellation of the factors listed above will often come into play. Let us look at two contrasting cases:

A. She is thirty, attractive, self-assured, and a successful businesswoman. She has her own apartment in a large city. She readily acknowledges — indeed, speaks with pride of — her homosexual orientation. She vaguely remembers having difficulty achieving orgasm during her early teens, but never subsequently. She has been homosexually active since age fifteen. It is extremely unlikely that psychological factors will interfere with her ability to achieve orgasm — especially while her situation remains the same.

B. She is seventeen, and no one she knows regards her as attractive. She is a high school student who has a difficult time getting even passing grades. She has little confidence in herself socially, academically, or in any other way.

She lives with her parents, who wonder why she is not more interested in boys — and who have made a number of pointed remarks about her seeming to be a "tomboy." The fact is, she has no sexual interest whatever in boys; they simply do not appeal to her. All her sexual fantasies involve other girls. But she wishes that this were not so. Given a magic wand, she would transform herself into a ravishingly beautiful girl whom boys found irresistible — and who was avidly interested in them.

She was raised to think of sex as "dirty." For as long as she can remember, the subject was never even alluded to in her house without snickering or embarrassment. She first attempted masturbation in her early teens, but she had been taught it was sinful so she tried hard to resist whenever she got the urge. She achieved orgasm a few times, but the "feeling" was never very powerful. After a while, she masturbated much less frequently.

She has had "crushes" on quite a few girls at school and made advances toward several of them. The advances were spurned, and on two occasions the girls spoke abusively to her, calling her a "queer" and a "dyke." Later, she was approached by an older girl. She did not find this girl attractive, but she was curious about what sex would be like. She enjoyed having the girl perform cunnilingus on her, but she did not enjoy reciprocating. She did not achieve orgasm.

Later she had encounters with several of this girl's friends. She did not find any of them especially appealing. To get aroused with them, she would entertain fantasies of other girls. One encounter took place in the home of her partner's parents, another in a garage, another in a parked car. She was never really comfortable; she always was concerned that she would be caught and reported to her family.

She never really felt good about having sex with these girls. She felt as if she were in some way confirming or reinforcing her homosexuality; she felt as though by not abstaining she were helping to ensure that her potential for heterosexual relationships would be irredeemably lost.

During the sex acts she wondered why she was not enjoying herself more than she did, why she was not even approaching orgasm. A few times it seemed that the "feeling" might be starting to develop inside her belly, but it promptly vanished. Nothing she did could bring it back. She began to worry that she might be sexually deformed. Maybe she was some sort of freak of nature. Maybe she would never have a satisfactory sex life with men or with other women.

Clearly, in both cases a multiplicity of influences seems to be guaranteeing perpetuation of the status quo — if not intensification of the situation. The more that Ms. A continues to enjoy sex and her homosexual life-style, the greater the likelihood that she will continue to enjoy both in the future. Likewise, the more frustration that Ms. B encounters, the more likely it is that her future attempts at sexual satisfaction will be frustrated.

How can one break this sort of vicious circle? The first step, it would seem, is acceptance of one's homosexual appetites. The next is to begin reconstructing one's circumstances so that homosexual relationships can be pursued in a comfortable, guilt-free atmosphere. This will often mean relocating in a city where parents, relatives, and childhood friends are not nearby to scold with their glances, their innuendos, their silences.

In a city with a large homosexually active population, the likelihood will be much greater of meeting people whom one finds appealing. Having sex with one or more such people — in comfortable surroundings, without fear of exposure or embarrassment — surely will be more enjoyable than sex was "back home." And the more enjoyable it is, the greater is the likelihood of easily achieved, satisfying orgasm. Once such an orgasm has been achieved, the prospects of additional ones improve. The better subsequent ones get, and the more easily they are achieved, the better are the prospects that future ones will be enjoyable and easily achieved.

If a woman has reason to suspect that she may suffer physical impediments to orgasm, we recommend a gynecological examination. If genital lesions are discovered, they can be remedied with simple surgery. In very rare cases, the examination may reveal a tumor or some other problem that is serious or at least potentially serious. Unfortunate though it is to have such a discovery made, it is much better to make the discovery early in the course of the condition's development, while there is still time to treat it.

In the vast majority of cases, the problem will be psychological. This is especially likely if the woman achieves orgasm at least occasionally, whether by masturbation, heterosexual stimulation, or homosexual stimulation. Some women may under these circumstances wish to pursue professional counseling.

Probably the best thing to do is masturbate regularly. This will teach a woman which types of stimuli make it easiest for her to achieve orgasm. She can then seek these same stimuli during relations with a partner. Masturbation can help develop what sexologists William H. Masters and Virginia E. Johnson have called "the orgasm habit." The studies of these two researchers suggest that the more frequently a person achieves orgasm, by whatever means, the better equipped that person is to achieve future orgasms by *any* means.

Male — Impotence

Impotence appears to be a much more complicated problem among homosexually active men than failure to achieve orgasm is among homosexually active women. This is not to say that impotence is not complicated also for men whose activity is exclusively heterosexual. However, while just about all the heterosexual problems also exist in homosexual relations, not all the homosexual problems exist in heterosexual relations. Here are some of the more common psychological influences:

GUILT

As with homosexually active women or heterosexually active people of either gender, guilt can be a serious problem for homosexually active men. However, it is probably more prevalent and more intense among homosexually active men, especially those with relatively little homosexual experience.

Many men believe that homosexual relations are morally wrong. Many are unable to accept the image of being a "homosexual." In addition, there is a vast array of societal abuses, ranging from the "fag jokes" of nightclub comedians to the vigilante attitudes of poorly informed parents who see every homosexually active person as a peril to a son's or daughter's heterosexuality.

As few readers of this book need be told, it takes considerable personal strength to maintain one's equanimity in the face of the vicious attacks directed at "the love that dares not speak its name." Plagued by feelings that one is doing something that one should not be doing — whether the prohibition is on moral, social, or other grounds — many men find themselves incapable of getting or sustaining an erection during homosexual acts. The problem is especially prevalent among relative newcomers to homosexual encounters, particularly if one's partner is a "forbidden" person — for example, someone much younger or someone with no previous homosexual experience — or if one fears being compromised. The problem grows more acute if some of the factors listed below are also present.

FEAR OF FAILURE

This is probably even more problematic among men than among women, because the woman need not actively maintain an erection: her physical participation in the act may proceed uninterruptedly, no matter what is going on in her mind, and she may eventually relax and have an orgasm. If a man fails to sustain an erection once, it is likely that he will approach the next act wondering if he will also fail this time. It may well be that the last failure resulted from an extraordinary circumstance — fear of discovery in a less than private place, overconsumption of alcohol, or illness. Nonetheless, the man may doubt his ability. His doubt makes him an observer as well as a participant in the act. This distracts him from the stimulation he should be experiencing. If his erection diminishes, his doubt increases. This may lead to complete loss of erection. And the next time, he has two "failures" to worry about instead of one. The vicious circle develops, failure begetting self-doubt and self-doubt begetting failure.

LACK OF INTEREST IN A PARTNER

This may be even more problematic among men than among women, who, as has been noted, can participate physically despite their lack of interest and who may, in the course of their participation, become aroused. The same circumstances that impel women to pursue relationships with people whom they do not find sexually attractive also impel men. A series of erectile failures with partners one does not find attractive can — and often will — make a man wonder about his potency and fear failure in future encounters.

INHIBITING SURROUNDINGS AND APPARENTLY IRRELEVANT DISTRACTIONS

As with women, these can also plague men — but with more devastating effect, for the woman may continue her sexual participation and perhaps think her way past the inhibiting factors, whereas the man must actively sustain his erection.

Contrary to the situation with women, who have homosexual orgasm problems relatively rarely, one or more of the above factors will frequently come into play with homosexually active men. Indeed, potency problems are probably much more common among the homosexually active than among those whose activity is exclusively heterosexual. If a man wishes to keep his activity secret, his problems are compounded. If he desires relationships with men he does not find particularly attractive — for example, with older men whose achievement, kindness, understanding, social station, or financial resources make the relationship desirable despite absence of attractiveness — impotence may be especially problematic. If he is worried about contracting venereal disease — as has been noted, an extremely serious matter among men who have many partners — potency problems may be compounded further.

As with women, some men will have few or none of these problems, while others will suffer a great many of them. If we could construct a profile of a man most likely to have the smallest number of these problems, he would probably be someone in his twenties who has been homosexually active for at least ten years and is fully accepting of his homosexual orientation; he would be in a career where he can openly acknowledge his orientation without fear of unfavorable treatment; he would live in a city that has a large homosexually active population, and his family would either accept his life-style or would be living in another city; he would have his own apartment or share one with a lover or someone who had no conflict with his life-style; he would not have financial worries, health worries, distracting work-related problems, or a history of potency failures in the recent past.

A man most likely to have the greatest number of these problems would probably be over forty and troubled about his homosexual desires; he would rather not have these desires and may indeed have undergone professional counseling in an attempt to get rid of them; he would probably think of homosexual activity as morally wrong and socially undesirable; he would be in a career where he could not dare reveal himself to be homosexually active; possibly he would be married to a woman who does not know about his homosexual orientation and would not accept the fact if she did; possibly he would have children, parents, siblings, other family members, and longtime personal acquaintances who would be appalled by his behavior; he would live in a small town that is quite distant from any city with a large homosexually active population, and he would be limited in his choice of partners to younger men who are hesitant if not unwilling to engage in homosexual acts; he would not have his own apartment and would thus have to limit his encounters to automobiles, the outdoors, etc.; on the few occasions when he might find a partner who was willing to provide stimulation as well as accept it, the man we are profiling would probably have a history of potency failures related to overexcitement as well as fear of failure, and he would now be all the more fearful of failure (and therefore all the more likely to distract himself from arousing stimuli); he might also have financial and/or health worries and/or distracting work-related problems.

Clearly, in both cases, the various influences conspire to guarantee perpetuation if not intensification of the status quo. The more the first man continues to enjoy sex and his homosexual life-style, the greater the likelihood that he will enjoy both even more in the future. The more problems and frustrations the second man encounters, the more likely it is that his future acts will be even more troublesome and frustrating.

How can one break the vicious circle? As with women, the first step is accepting one's homosexual appetites. The next is to begin reconstructing one's circumstances so that homosexual relationships can be pursued in a comfortable, guilt-free atmosphere. This may mean relocating in a distant city and perhaps even pursuing another occupation. Many men will not want to make these sacrifices, especially after the age of forty, and accordingly will continue to suffer the status quo or may even halt homosexual activity completely. However, others may reflect that they are entering what is probably the last half of their sex life and may therefore be more highly motivated; they may even opt for dramatic changes in circumstances — such as divorcing a wife of many years and leaving a prosperous career — because they want to seek fulfillment "while there's still time."

Of course, not all impotence is induced by psychological factors. If a man cannot achieve erection under any circumstance, even masturbation, there is a good possibility that his problem is physical. If impotence is a relatively recent development, the likelihood is even greater that the problem is physical, especially if there are no obvious circumstantial factors that seem to be responsible.

Here are some physical causes of impotence:

• Cancer of the penis and/or surgical treatment of cancer of the penis — Cancer of the skin of the penis represents 1 to 2 percent of all cancers in the male. It is believed to be less frequent among men who are circumcised. The usual site is beneath the foreskin, and irritation in that moist environment may be what caused or encouraged the tumor's development. If you cannot retract the foreskin, it should be retracted surgically so that the area may be inspected. Any wart-like ulcerated growth should be examined. A biopsy will reveal whether it is cancerous.

If the growth is small, simple circumcision might remove the entire cancerous area. In more advanced cases, x-radiation and surgical removal of part or all of the penis may be necessary. This can usually be avoided if the growth is detected early; therefore, any suspicious penile lesion should be investigated promptly.

The tumor itself may in rare cases cause impotence, either by interfering with the erectile tissues in the penis or by causing pain when the foreskin resists erectile growth. More often, the man will remain potent until the growth is removed. If erectile tissue must be cut away to remove the cancer, permanent impotence may follow.

• Trauma to the penis — Erectile tissue may be damaged traumatically. Physicians have treated traumas incurred under such circumstances as the following:

A was working at a construction job. He controlled a winch lift that operated by winding a cable on a cylinder. He moved close to the cylinder while it was in motion, and the fly of his pants became entwined in the cable. He was pulled into the coils and, by the time the machine could be stopped, the skin of his penis had been stripped off like that of a banana.

B, a butcher, accidentally let his knife slip and cut almost completely across the penis.

C, while under the influence of LSD, injected his penis with an analgesic. The erectile tissues were completely destroyed.

D got involved in a fight with his lover, who tried literally to amputate D's penis with a kitchen knife. The organ was not severed, but damage to the erectile tissue was irreparable.

Once the erectile tissue of the penis is cut or otherwise damaged, there is no known method to reestablish the delicate sponge-like cells that absorb blood, thus causing erection. If damage has been only partial, erection may still be possible — aided, perhaps, by implant of a silicone splint. However, most often, the damage is total and impotence permanent.

It is possible that microsurgical repair techniques and even penis transplants may ultimately become commonplace. However, the technology for both appears from this juncture to be far in the future.

• Surgery to organs of the genitourinary system — A number of genitourinary surgical procedures will cause irreversible impotence by severing nerves that transmit sexual impulses or by damaging the erectile tissue or the arteries that supply it with blood. These procedures generally are undertaken to remove cancerous or benign tumors.

Removal of the urinary bladder, the prostate gland, or the lymph glands that lie along the dorsal wall of the body (in the retroperitoneal space) will always cause irreversible impotence. If a prostatic tumor is not malignant (cancerous) the usual procedure is removal of only part of the gland. In these cases, impotence need not result. Generally, older patients are more likely to be impotent after the operation than younger patients. However, patients who retain their potency do develop a condition called retrograde ejaculation. At orgasm, the semen does not flow out of the urethra but rather runs backwards into the urinary bladder. This results from removal of or interference with the ejaculatory ducts. The sensations of orgasm remain the same; the only difference is absence of an ejaculate. This means that the person cannot sire children, but at the age when prostatic disease normally presents itself (usually over fifty, often over seventy), this is rarely a consideration. If a man wants to sire children, there are surgical approaches that can correct retrograde ejaculation.

Sometimes surgery done in the intestinal tract will lead to impotence if the area removed is extensive and involves encroachment on nerves or vessels involved in sexual function. Surgical repair of the main artery in the body the aorta, which extends from the heart to the various terminals of other arterial systems, can result in impotence. X-ray therapy of cancer of the prostate may also cause or encourage impotence; studies suggest that about one man in three will be impotent after these treatments.

• Peyronie's disease — In this disease, a stony-hard, elongated mass develops about half an inch under the skin of the anterior surface of the penis. The mass is composed of disk-shaped plaques that are localized in various areas of the erectile tissue and usually joined along one side of the penis. As the mass grows, the penis bends sharply. Erection becomes so painful that sexual arousal is impossible. The mass can become so dense that calcium develops within the area. The effect is as if a bone were developing within the penis.

The cause of Peyronie's disease is not known. Researchers speculate that it may result in some chemical way from one or more venereal diseases, from trauma, from viral infection (not necessarily sexually transmitted), or from the escape into the erectile tissue of urine from the urethra, causing inflammation and scar tissue. In any case, the disease probably starts as an inflammation of the arteries in the area of the penis immediately above the urethra; this then produces scar tissue, and the penis becomes bent.

The first symptom generally is an awareness that the penis is becoming bent. Pain may develop along with this bending or sometimes even before bending is visible. A sufferer may say that during sexual relations he feels as if the point of a pin were being jabbed into his skin along the side of the penis. Sometimes nodules may be felt beneath the penile skin.

Diagnosis is made by finding the characteristic plaques beneath the skin. This is one of the few diseases that produces foreign matter on which a biopsy should not be performed. A biopsy may aggravate the development of scar tissue.

Mysteriously, in some patients the disease vanishes as unexpectedly as it arrives. More often, pain will increase to the point where treatment is demanded.

The most prevalent treatment is surgical removal of the scar tissue. A piece of skin from the abdomen is placed in the area. When this heals, the patient may be restored to normal erectile function. However, the failure rate is substantial: we estimate close to 50 percent.

In some instances a surgeon, instead of literally cutting out the scar tissue, will use a high speed dental drill to remove it. It was thought that this approach would lessen damage to surrounding tissue and thus result in fewer post-operative potency problems. However, results appear to be about the same as when actual cutting is done.

Numerous medications have been employed in attempts at chemotherapy. The most widely prescribed appear to be vitamin E and a vitamin B6 agent, potassium p-aminobenzoate. X-radiation, diathermy, heat treatments, massage, stretching of the area, electrical treatments, and injection of various chemicals directly into the tissue have also been tried. With none of them does the success rate appear to be significantly higher than with placebo, that is, no treatment or an irrelevant "treatment" (such as a sugar pill) that the patient believes will be effective.

• Priapism — The term describes a long-lasting erection that is not related to sexual stimulation. Usually it lasts for several days or weeks, then diminishes, leaving the man impotent. It is intensely painful because the blood that normally enters the penis only during erection continues to fill and over-distend the organ.

Obviously priapism results from some sort of damage to the mechanisms that supply the penis with blood. It will occur with any condition that causes blood within the penis to clot. However, except for obvious situations such as penile trauma, the reasons for this clotting or for the unexpected penile engorgement with blood are not clear.

The condition has been linked statistically with sickle cell anemia, syphilis, leukemia, and various tumors; however, it is not clear to researchers how these diseases could cause or encourage priapism.

Many treatments have been attempted, including spinal anesthesia, general anesthesia, injections of various medications into the penis, drainage of blood from the penis with needles, attachment of a vein from the thigh into the penis to drain the blood, and establishment of a new drainage passageway for blood to pass from one area to another within the penis. None has met with significant success. Once the delicate internal structures of the penis are damaged by clotting, they apparently cannot be returned to normal function.

• General medical diseases — Any disease that upsets the chemical or hormonal balance of the body can cause or encourage impotence. Especially prominent among these are diseases of the adrenal glands (e.g., Addison's disease), the testicles (e.g., hypogonadism), the pituitary (e.g., acromegaly), the thyroid, the kidneys, and the liver. Sometimes if the disease itself does not cause impotence, the treatment of it will. For example, dialysis, the method by which the blood is cleared of waste products when the kidneys fail, destroys the ability to achieve erection, as does administration of female hormones, common in the treatment of cancer of the prostate.

Various neurologic conditions can cause impotence. These include diseases that affect the central nervous system, congenital defects of the spinal cord, lesions that disrupt the sexual integration center of the spinal cord, and syphilis of the brain or spinal cord.

Any disease that prevents blood from getting into the penis will cause impotence. The list of such diseases is virtually unending, for almost any disease can lead to diminished flow of blood. Anemia and other conditions that bring about fatigue or weakness are the most prominent culprits.

Diabetes may in certain advanced cases cause impotence. Diabetes is a disease of the pancreas and blood vessels that prevents the body from obtaining the insulin it needs to control the blood sugar level. Its cause is unknown. Its cardinal symptoms are increased thirst, hunger, and urination.

• Drugs — Many medications block the ganglia, or nerve impulse transmission centers, that control the erection mechanism. These include medications used to control high blood pressure. One of them, Aldomet (generic name: methyldopate), may, at certain times, make erection impossible, while another, Ismelin (guanethidine sulfate), does not interfere with erection but may inhibit ejaculation. Such psychoactive drugs as Thorazine (phenothiazine), Tofranil (imipramine hydrochloride), Valium (diazepam), Librium (chlordiazepoxide), Mellaril (thioridazine), and Pondimin (fenfluramine hydrochloride) may also inhibit erection or ejaculation or may diminish sexual desire. Potency generally returns when the medication is suspended.

Heroin and other narcotics, alcohol, marijuana, and LSD may also inhibit erection, ejaculation, and/or sex drive, though they by no means always do so; some people report increased sex drive and ability while under the influence of the nonnarcotic members of this group.

Impotence might be called a symptom in search of a disease. In a very real sense, it can be a symptom of just about any bodily or emotional disorder. Determining its cause is particularly difficult because sexual potency is by no means an inevitable "normal" phenomenon. In other words, erections do not merely happen; they must be stimulated. Barriers to stimulation include not only a man's own physical and emotional problems but also the ineptness (physical, emotional, intellectual) of a partner.

Given the many diseases of which impotence may serve as a symptom, it is a good idea to consult a urologist promptly if circumstantial factors do not seem to be responsible. This would be especially important if one is impotent with several consecutive partners after a long history of no potency problems.

Male — Hasty Ejaculation

How fast is too fast? Some theoreticians regard ejaculation as "premature" if it takes place before a partner can achieve orgasm, or before an arbitrary period of time (say two minutes, or three, or five). Other researchers, among them the late Dr. Alfred C. Kinsey, have argued that rapid ejaculation is a sign of sexual vigor in every mammalian species, including the human, and that ejaculation should be deemed "premature" only if it takes place before intromission. Between these poles are all sorts of opinions and definitions, embracing such criteria as the statistically average ejaculation time of all men and the statistically average ejaculation time of the ejaculating individual himself.

From a medical standpoint, the last criterion is most important. Thus, for our purposes, a man may be said to ejaculate prematurely if he ejaculates *considerably sooner than he ordinarily would.* The word "considerably," of course, invites further discussion. Suffice it to say that the man himself might be deemed the best judge of whether he is ejaculating "considerably," or significantly, sooner than normal. If he thinks he has a problem, he has a problem.

Premature ejaculation, as defined above, may be a sequela of prostate disorder. The exact mechanism by which this comes about is not clear, but in some cases of prostate disorder, premature ejaculation is a prominent symptom. Thus, when a man finds himself ejaculating considerably sooner than he ordinarily would, it is a good idea, we think, to investigate the prostate — especially if the episodes of premature ejaculation are consecutive and of sudden onset.

That having been said, the fact is that relatively few men really ejaculate "prematurely" in terms of the above definition. Granted, many would like to ejaculate less quickly than they presently do. But failure to live up to one's ideals (whether physical, intellectual, or in some other realm) does not necessarily constitute a medical condition. Care should be taken to differentiate between the medical concept of *premature* ejaculation and what is merely *quick* ejaculation.

A young man with limited experience might reasonably be expected to ejaculate rather quickly, perhaps even before intromission, the first time he attempts sexual union with someone he finds extremely attractive. A man who has been sexually continent for a long period — for instance, someone hospitalized for abdominal surgery — might ejaculate hastily when he resumes sex relations after leaving the hospital. This is not *premature* ejaculation in any medical sense; it is merely quick ejaculation, related to the person's current situation. As the situation changes, so, we assume, will his ejaculatory response.

Care also should be taken not to regard as premature an

ejaculatory pattern that is merely the result of a nervous system's being more finely tuned than that of the average man. This topic merits exploration.

Erection and ejaculation are frequently thought of as inextricably linked, but actually they are independent processes. Just as a man can have an erection without ejaculating, so can he ejaculate without an erection. Each process is under the control of a different area of the nervous system, and both are responsive to psychological as well as physical stimuli.

The penis can become erect by wholly mental processes: looking at a person or merely fantasying about that person. Likewise, wholly physical arousal is possible: fondling the penis may cause erection even in the absence of mental stimulation. Of course, the most effective stimulation combines the physical and the mental. The other side of this coin is that erection can likewise be prevented by either physical or mental processes or by both working in harmony — ask the man who has lost an erection from lack of stimulation by a lethargic partner or from hearing a key turn in the door of the next hotel room.

Similarly, ejaculation can be controlled by mental or physical forces or by both working in harmony. Many men find that they can accelerate or retard ejaculation by changing the rhythm or angle of intromission, or by fantasying sex with a different partner, or by deliberately forcing sexual thoughts from their minds. Experiments with laboratory animals have identified an ejaculatory center which, when stimulated electronically, results in ejaculation without erection. A similar ejaculatory center almost certainly exists in men. Just as some people have superior nerve reflexes, as measured in a pilot's or automobile driver's reaction time, so too, apparently, some people have a faster-than-average sexual reaction time.

Behavioral scientists frequently ascribe all cases of quick or slow ejaculation to emotional causes — emotional "immaturity," whatever that is supposed to mean, or "dependency" or "emotional inadequacy." However, the evidence developed thus far suggests that physical factors may play a role as great as or even greater than that of emotional factors.

How are problems of ejaculatory timing treated? Genuine

premature ejaculation linked to prostatic causes — very rare — is treated as part of the prostate problem: the disease is cured (by antibiotics or other therapy) and the problem of premature ejaculation vanishes. Long-standing quick ejaculation, as opposed to the medical concept of premature ejaculation, until recently has been something of an enigma for which sexologists have prescribed, with varying degrees of success, such disparate therapies as anesthetic ointments, yoga-like concentration efforts, tranquilizers, small quantities of alcohol, aspirin, and a host of other techniques or agents. However, in 1970, Masters and Johnson introduced techniques in their book *Human Sexual Inadequacy* that proved almost 100 percent successful in helping men achieve ejaculatory control.

Masters and Johnson blame hasty ejaculation (when physical causes have been ruled out) on such conditioning factors in the male's adolescence and early adulthood as harried encounters in automobiles or other uncomfortable places where there is constant pressure to "finish" so that the couple will not be discovered. An important factor in overcoming hasty ejaculation, these researchers contend, is establishing precisely the opposite atmosphere for a man's present sexual relations — an atmosphere where the man is confident that his partner is enjoying the experience and seeks to prolong it for as long as both partners desire it. However, a change in ambience alone may not be enough to decondition the male in whom hasty ejaculation has become a deeply ingrained response. To assist in deconditioning, Masters and Johnson employ a series of exercises developed by Dr. William Semans at Duke University in North Carolina.

The exercises were developed for heterosexual couples, but they can also be employed homosexually. We will describe them here as performed by A, who seeks to delay his ejaculation, and B, the partner who wants to help him achieve that objective.

In the first exercise, B sits with his back against the headboard of a bed and his legs spread wide; A lies on his back between B's legs; A's head is toward the foot of the bed, his legs bracket B's hips, and his buttocks are against B's thighs so that B has easy access to his penis. B now fondles A until A is fully erect. Then, immediately, B firmly squeezes the head of A's penis between his thumb and first two fingers. The thumb is placed on the frenulum, on the ventral surface of the penis just below the coronal ridge, and the first and second fingers on the dorsal surface bracketing the coronal ridge.

Intense pressure is applied for about three seconds. This causes A to lose not only all urge to ejaculate but also — usually — 10 to 30 percent of his full erection. B then waits about twenty seconds, after which he resumes fondling the penis. When A again achieves full erection, B again employs the squeeze technique. The pattern is repeated until A ejaculates. Generally four or five repetitions are possible during the first training session, and a substantially higher number during subsequent sessions.

In the second exercise, A lies on his back and B positions himself over A. The partners decide whether anal intercourse or fellatio should be performed. B's position will be whatever facilitates performance of the desired act.

After bringing A to erection and performing the squeeze technique two or three times, B introduces A's penis into B's mouth or anus. B then remains motionless until A indicates that his excitement is about to go out of control. B thereupon withdraws from the penis and employs the squeeze technique again. When A has regained full control, intromission is reestablished.

Subsequently, as A learns to withhold orgasm during periods of intromission, he is encouraged to engage in pelvic thrusting while B remains motionless. As A's control increases over a number of sessions, B begins actively stimulating A. Eventually, the couple is able to perform in whatever position both partners find desirable.

In certain cases of hasty ejaculation linked to emotional or situational factors, sexologists have reported failures in therapy; however, the vast majority of emotional and situational cases are fully and quickly remediable. Masters and Johnson report only five failures among 186 heterosexual couples. This rate — less than 3 percent — is extraordinary for treatment of any behavioral or psychological related problem. However, there is no reason that it should not be as effective among homosexual couples as among those whose activity is exclusively heterosexual.

Sexual Stimulants and Sexual Aids ─────────────

When confronted with sexual problems, people often seek help from medications and foods. Let us look at some of the foods and medications that are said to be of value.

• Testosterone (the male hormone) — Many medications containing testosterone are used in treating impotent men. Unfortunately, testosterone does not restore potency except when men are deficient in the hormone. This deficiency as a basis for impotency is rare.

In many cases men seem to improve sexually after a testosterone injection, but in most cases this probably is a result of placebo effect: getting better because you believe you have just taken a medication that will make you get better.

Some physicians have observed that when homosexually active men are given testosterone, they tend to become anxious — whereas men whose activity is exclusively heterosexual do not. Whether this is factual or fanciful remains open to question.

• Vitamin E (tocopherol) — Vitamin E was discovered in 1922 by researchers H. M. Evans and K. S. Bishop. In the more than half a century since, finding any two physicians who agree completely on the function and value of the vitamin has been difficult. In 1967, the *Journal of the American Medical Association* ran an editorial headlined, "Vitamin in Search of a Disease." The search, it would seem, is still going on.

Some researchers assert that the vitamin has no value, sexual or otherwise. Others claim it does many things. Biochemist E. V. Shute of Canada claims that his research supports that vitamin E has the following actions:

(1) Prevents thrombosis in the human blood stream

(2) Protects from oxygen within the body certain materials, such as vitamin C and various co-enzymes

(3) Prevents excessive formation of scar tissue

(4) Dilates (opens more widely) the blood vessels

(5) Helps keep the red blood cells healthy

Vitamin E has been hailed as an aphrodisiac, owing probably to animal studies in which rats who were deprived of the vitamin developed sperm that did not move (immotile sperm). Later on damage developed in the tissue that produces the sperm. However, while animal experiments are often of predictive value for humans, the fact is that impotent men to whom vitamin E is administered rarely if ever show improved potency to a greater degree than can be explained by placebo effect.

Conceivably some people may have a vitamin E deficiency that encourages impotence and may regain potency when they take large quantities of the vitamin, but the best available evidence suggests that vitamin E is of no value in treating sexual problems.

• Pumpkin seeds — Many health-food books have encouraged pumpkin seed consumption as a potency aid. The reasoning is that pumpkin seeds are rich in zinc, which is present in large amounts in the prostate gland, prostatic secretions, and spermatazoa. Its function in these organs and media is not known.

We do know that zinc helps in wound healing. Patients given zinc supplements after surgery were found to heal faster than people without zinc supplements. But there is no evidence that this metal is of any help to the impotent.

• Iodine — Shellfish have long been valued as an aphrodisiac. This owes to their high content of iodine. If a person has a deficiency in iodine, which is needed by the thyroid gland, he may indeed overcome that deficiency and in the process improve his sexual performance. However, there does not seem to be any evidence that iodine can be of sexual value to people who do not suffer a deficiency.

• Amyl nitrate — Nitrates and nitrites have long been used as sexual stimulants. "Poppers," as they are sometimes called, come in small glass cylinders. To use them, one generally breaks the cylinder inside a handkerchief and inhales the strong-smelling fumes. This dilates the blood vessels and causes a rapid drop in blood pressure — an important service for sufferers of coronary artery disease, for whom these drugs are intended by their developers.

The theory behind using the medication for sexual performance is that dilation of the blood vessels will aid blood flow to the penis, thus improving erections and sexual feeling. The potency effect is almost surely psychological. The relatively small amount of amyl nitrate inhaled almost certainly is not sufficient to increase blood flow into the penis. Perhaps, however, the drop in blood pressure in some way intensifies sexual sensation. In any case, this drop in blood pressure is followed by headaches and increased pressure in the fluid of the eyes. This can have disastrous effects on a person who has a weakness — whether or not discovered — in the pertinent bodily systems. A drop in blood pressure could cause a stroke, and an elevation of eye pressure might start a bout of glaucoma. We strongly advise against using nitrates or nitrites except for medical purposes under a physician's supervision.

• Ginseng — This is the name of a plant discovered in Quebec in the early eighteenth century and in the Orient some years earlier. Its root is widely used in the Far East, and especially Korea, as an aphrodisiac. Either it is ingested whole or is brewed as tea. It is presently a popular item in so-called health food shops in North America.

Present scientific evidence neither confirms nor challenges the claim that this root or its derivatives have sexual value.

• "Spanish fly" is neither Spanish nor a fly but rather a compound made up of the ground bodies of certain beetles found in Europe and Africa. The matured insect is bright green and caught in June or July. The trees in which these beetles live are beaten with sticks and the insects caught as they fall to the ground. They are then placed into a diluted vinegar solution and later dried, ground, and used as a powder.

The resultant "medicine" is a poison. It can be — and has been — fatal to people who have taken even extremely small doses for aphrodisiac purposes.

It produces blisters and blebs in the urinary tract. In women, this irritation is so severe that it often triggers feelings very much like those of intense sexual arousal. In men, "Spanish fly" can produce a painful "mechanical" erection like that of priapism, stimulated by blood flow rather than sexual desire. While people who are in this state will often be extremely aroused sexually, there is no evidence that they enjoy sex more. In any case, the dangers of the drug are such that few people who know about them would consider using it recreationally.

• Acupuncture — This form of treatment involves placing needles into the skin in order to stimulate or block a widespread network of nerves that is said to exist under the skin. The network supposedly carries impulses to and from "deeper" body structures, such as the heart, lungs, and brain.

Such qualifiers as "supposedly" and "is said to" are employed because no one has ever demonstrated the network of nerves — or "meridians," as acupuncturists term them — on which the treatment is based. At the same time, results observed among acupuncturists suggest that *something* definitely happens when the needles are applied. One Western scientist based in the East, Dr. Peter Lisowski, professor of anatomy at the University of Hong Kong, theorizes that some sort of neurohormonal mechanism may be involved.

Results of acupuncture therapy for sexual problems were presented at a Russian Acupuncture Conference at Gorki. Of thirty-five cases of physical sexual malfunction treated, twenty-six were reported cured or improved. Of these, twenty-four returned for examination a year and a half later. Of these, twenty-one remained cured or improved.

Encouraging though these figures may seem, the fact remains that reports of "improvement" or "cure" are difficult to assess and even more difficult to ascribe to a particular treatment. Cardiologist E. Grey Diamond, who visited China in 1973 and observed acupuncture in a variety of settings, and Paul Gillette, who went there a year later on fundamentally the same mission, were both told by many Chinese specialists in acupuncture that these scientists believed a great many if not most recipients of the treatment were experiencing placebo effect.

As Dr. Diamond has noted, acupuncture is a relatively harmless placebo, if placebo it is. Still, it is not — at least not on the basis of the present evidence — a verifiable therapy for impotence or any other problem in sexual performance.

CHAPTER 21

Gay Preventive and Curative Medicine

The surest preventive of sexual disease and injury is abstinence — which raises the question of whether the prevention is worse than the occurrence. Obviously, few readers would feel they had struck a felicitous bargain if the price of sexual health were lifelong celibacy.

The next surest preventive of sexual disease is monogamy, which some may find only slightly less odious. However, as has been noted, if both partners are disease-free when the relationship begins, the chances of contracting V.D. subsequently are virtually nil. As additional partners get involved with either of the original partners, the likelihood of venereal infection increases not merely arithmetically but exponentially.

Some years ago, Robert Rowan began noting the number of his homosexually active urologic patients who reported monogamous relationships. The nonmonogamous outnumbered the monogamous, two to one. This could be interpreted as evidence that, in general, homosexually active men tend to have multiple relationships and, indeed, some sexologists have drawn that conclusion from published statistics of patients going to V.D. clinics. However, we think it more likely that the preponderance of nonmonogamous patients reflects the fact that *these are the people who most often contract sexually related disease.* Rowan has also found among patients whose activity is exclusively heterosexual that the nonmonogamous tend to contract sexually transmitted disease about twice as often as the monogamous.

In any case, monogamy obviously will not protect you against sexual injury. The only sure preventive of anorectal damage is avoidance of anorectal penetration. If anorectal penetration is undertaken, use Vaseline, K-Y Jelly, or some other lubricant before penetration. Gentle and gradual anorectal dilatation, combined with a lubricant, will afford some protection to the anal sphincter and the rectal walls. The lubricant should be applied profusely and with gentle, thorough massaging before penetration takes place. Additional quantities should be applied during sex when friction is felt.

The insertion of foreign bodies poses serious danger of injury to the rectal walls and/or of loss of the item into the rectum.

Enemas should be avoided. The problem, however, is having the rectum empty for penetration. If you cannot evacuate the channel without an enema, plain water is the safest material to use. This should empty the bowel without placing an undue burden on the anorectal structures.

If you do not choose to be monogamous, the next best preventive of venereal infection in men is the condom. This device does not completely eliminate the risk of V.D., but it reduces the odds considerably.

Men are often surprised when told that condoms prevent homosexual transmission of venereal infection, probably because they relate the device to contraception. However, there is no doubt that a condom offers the best mechanical barrier to sexual transmission of disease. Many men dislike using a condom because it inhibits sensation, disrupts mood, or causes embarrassment. ("I'm afraid the other guy will think I'm some kind of freak or that I don't trust him.") On the brighter side, people whose last exposure to a condom was ten or more years ago probably will be pleasantly surprised to find that products in current manufacture are considerably thinner and less sensation-inhibiting than those in the supposedly good-old-days.

People sometimes ask about "pro-kits," which they associate with military V.D. prevention programs. It is true that such kits were used during the Second World War. They contained an antiseptic material which was injected into the urethra after sexual relations to kill any V.D. bacteria that may have entered the passageway. They are no longer available, because they were found ineffective. They were painful to use and rejected by most people. Men who did use them according to instructions probably avoided some gonorrhea and N.S.U., but not other sexually transmitted diseases. In any case, "pro-kits" are no longer being manufactured.

Men sometimes ask if they can avoid V.D. by washing the penis with soap and/or by urinating after sexual relations. Don't count on it. Neither technique will prevent transmission of syphilis or gonorrhea or other venereally contracted diseases. The idea of urinating after penile intromission is to "wash out" infectious bacteria that may have entered the urethra. Experience indicates that many bacteria are not expelled this way. Conceivably, washing or urinating eliminates *some* bacteria, and therefore both practices may be preferable to doing nothing. However, neither can be relied on to prevent venereal disease.

People frequently ask if it is not possible to take an antibiotic regularly, or immediately before or after sex, to prevent transmission of disease. The reasoning is, if these antibiotics cure disease, surely they can also help prevent it.

They can. A relatively small number of physicians personally take one or another antibiotic before nonmonogamous relations. Why shouldn't patients take them also?

A very small number of physicians believe this is exactly the thing to do. Says Dr. Lonny Myers, vice president of the Midwest Association for the Study of Human Sexuality: "We prescribe maintenance doses of antibiotics for little children with rheumatic fever, for acne, and for a host of other ills. Why not prescribe them also for adults who run a relatively high risk of contracting venereal disease?" One answer is that repeated and prolonged use of antibiotics creates a sensitivity to these drugs. You might take penicillin (or tetracycline or another antibiotic) with absolutely no reaction dozens of times and then unexpectedly develop a reaction as a result of repeated dosages. There is no way to predict whether a reaction will take place, and it could be fatal. Even if it isn't fatal, once an allergy develops, a person can no longer safely take the drug. The next time you need it might be a life-or-death situation and you wouldn't be able to use it because you developed a sensitivity to it through anti-V.D. use. Most researchers take an only-when-needed approach to all drugs: use them if you must, but only if you must.

Another problem with using antibiotics prophylactically for V.D. is that resistant strains of bacteria can be created. In other words, repeated exposure to the drug (especially at doses too low to destroy the germ) can encourage development of bacteria that resist treatment. This has already occurred with certain strains of gonorrhea. If a person develops a resistant strain, different antibiotics must be tried until one is found that can overcome the disease. Eventually a strain may develop that resists all known therapeutic agents. If no treatment is found, the strain may prove fatal to many who have contracted it.

Still another problem with using antibiotics prophylactically for V.D. is that no one single drug works against all bacteria. Prophylactic penicillin, in adequate doses, can prevent syphilis and gonorrhea but not chancroid, L.G.V., granuloma inguinale, and other diseases. Drugs which, taken prophylactically, prevent these diseases don't work against syphilis and gonorrhea.

One way to avoid sexually transmitted disease is to know what to look for in your partner.

• Always be on the alert for a chancre — the ulcer, or sore, that characterizes syphilis or chancroid. It will usually be found on the penis, anus, lips, or nipples. Inspect under the foreskin of uncircumcised males: chancres are often found there.

Of course, it generally is deemed impolitic to approach one's partner in the manner of a military short-arm inspector. On the other hand, if you can manage to be surreptitiously on the lookout for these symptoms without offending the potential possessor of them, you can limit considerably your prospects of becoming infected.

• Any type of skin rash, particularly around the mouth or anus, may be secondary syphilis or other venereal diseases. If a partner has a rash, extreme caution is advisable. More specifically, avoid sexual contact unless you have a fully satisfactory explanation to the effect that the phenomenon is nonsexual.

• A urethral drip or discharge is a sure sign of danger. Avoid sex under all circumstances.

• Also be wary of a fever blister, herpes ("cold sore"), or any patch of small blisters or other lesions on the genitals, anus, mouth, or surface of the skin. These developments need not necessarily indicate V.D., but they often do.

Whatever precautions you take against contracting venereal disease, a good way to protect yourself against the diseases' most serious effects is to visit regularly a V.D. clinic or a private physician. If you or your usual partner tend to have considerable activity outside the relationship (say two or three outside partners per month), a monthly V.D. screening is a good idea. The fewer partners you have, the fewer screenings you'll need in the course of a year. If you're looking for a round figure, try one screening for every five partners, no matter what the time span.

Lists of clinics where V.D. tests are administered, often at no cost, appear in the appendices.

CHAPTER 22

Emotional Considerations

Probably the most prevalent emotional problem among people who experience homosexual desire is their unwillingness to accept that they are experiencing it. They believe that people should not desire sexual relations with others of the same gender. They believe that there is something wrong with those who do. These anxiety-producing beliefs are encouraged by many psychologists, psychiatrists, sociologists, and other accredited observers who have ventured opinions about homosexuality. They term it "abnormal," "unnatural," or some other word that suggests that a clinical judgment has been made to the effect that homosexuality is wrong.

What is needed here are the services of a good semanticist. Simple logic reveals that there can be no rights or wrongs — no "shoulds" — in matters of appetite. We may, as a matter of philosophy, decide that we should *behave* in certain ways, that it is immoral to behave otherwise. But appetites do not respond to moral suasion. They simply exist, wonderfully indifferent to our wishes regarding them.

The existence of homosexual appetite is extremely widespread, not only among humans but throughout the kingdom of mammals. Dr. J. P. Scott, of Jackson Memorial Laboratory in Bar Harbor, Maine, tells of an experiment in which two male sheep were placed on one side of a fence opposite a female in estrus; the males responded to the stimulation of the inaccessible female by "exhibiting courtship behavior toward each other." Dr. Frank A. Beach, in *Psychological Review*, writes of similar experiments in which isolated male rats — not subject to heterosexual stimulation — also related homosexually. In another experiment reported by Dr. Scott, a male dog who "responded normally to a female dog in estrus" was isolated temporarily in the company of a male cat. After a time, "the dog began licking its [the cat's] posterior; the cat now responded by assuming the position normally taken by a female in coitus. Both animals appeared to obtain some sexual satisfaction."

In one of the more interesting studies of homosexual desire among humans, psychologist John S. Yankowski surveyed, with parents' permission, certain male members of the seventh grade classes of twenty junior high schools. Each pupil completed anonymously a questionnaire on which, interspersed among general heterosexual and nonsexual queries, were items designed to reveal homosexual desire and the nature and extent of follow-up behavior. Three years later, those of the original group who had gone on to tenth grade in the same school district were questioned again. Two years after that, those who had advanced to twelfth grade in the same schools were questioned a third time.

Among the seventh graders, 85 percent said that they had at least once wanted to touch another boy's penis and 84 percent said they had gone ahead and done so. Meanwhile, 90 percent said they had permitted another boy to touch their penis but only 88 percent said they had wanted to be touched that way.

The figures for those who did the touching suggest a high degree of spontaneity and lack of inhibition — only one boy in a hundred refrained from acting out his desire to touch someone else. But the figures for the recipients of penile touching seem contradictory. How could it be that 90 boys in 100 were touched while only eighty-eight wanted to be?

It is possible, of course, that the reluctant 2 percent were coerced into permitting the touching. It is also possible that the disproportion results from pupils misunderstanding one or both items in the questionnaire. A third possibility, however — which seems most probable — is that the avowedly nondesirous were aware of social attitudes toward homosexuality and were trapped into lying by the language of the questions and the order in which they were asked. "Has another boy ever touched your sex organ?" does not preclude voluntary behavior, but neither does it suggest it. One might answer affirmatively and still escape the onus of being a "homosexual." But "Have you ever *wanted* another boy to touch your sex organ?" clearly establishes desire; the onus is there! Having in the first question truthfully admitted to homosexual participation, the avowedly nondesirous respondents, upon encountering the second question a good deal farther on in the questionnaire, either forgot their earlier answer and lied unthinkingly or else lied with the expectation that the contradiction would go unnoticed (erasures were prohibited).

Whatever the reasons for lying, a review of the responses of these same students as tenth graders suggests that lying is precisely what they did. Among the tenth grade respondents, 84 percent reported having been touched sometime in the past and 31 percent said they had been touched during the interval since the last questionnaire. But only 58 percent admitted to *desiring* being touched sometime in the past and the same 31 percent said they had desired it since the last questionnaire.

In other words, among boys who admitted that they continued to be recipients of homosexual touching after seventh grade, all reported that they wanted to be touched. Apparently those who had problems with the onus of homosexual desire either discontinued letting themselves be touched or reported that they had not been. Meanwhile, asked to recall activity over their lifetime, six boys in one hundred who as seventh graders reported being touched now changed their story, and thirty in one hundred who as seventh graders reported wanting to be touched now said they never had wanted it.

Among twelfth grade respondents, 72 percent reported having been touched sometime in the past, and 38 percent said they had been touched during the interval since the last questionnaire. Meanwhile, 73 percent admitted desiring being touched sometime in the past and 45 percent admitted desiring it since the last questionnaire.

In other words, a much greater number of boys reported having once been homosexually desirous than had done so in tenth grade. Almost all had translated that desire into action. Meanwhile, a relatively large number reported homosexual desire in the interval since tenth grade — and many but definitely not all of these fulfilled it.

The discrepancies between these figures and those of the tenth graders are extremely interesting. It is highly doubtful that an experience genuinely forgotten in the tenth grade would be recalled in the twelfth — especially by so many different boys. Possibly the respondents had managed to cast off feelings of shame about actions considered to be far in the past. Or perhaps they simply gained confidence in the anonymity of replies to the questionnaire and no longer were motivated to lie. In any case, a significant number of them had participated in — and an even larger number had desired — homosexual activity in the recent past.

None of this necessarily proves anything, but it strongly supports two points made elsewhere:

(1) Homosexual behavior is extremely widespread, at least until people discover that others do not approve of it;

(2) People learn very early in life that homosexual behavior is widely disapproved.

Here lies the crux of most emotional problems involving homosexuality: people want to have relationships and believe they shouldn't. Over the years, many apparently bring their behavior in line with their beliefs. But those who don't may believe that there is something "wrong" with them, that they are "sick."

We made the point in the Introduction that homosexual behavior *cannot* logically be perceived as illness. Let us say here that neither need it be problematic. If a person accepts his or her desires and the decision to gratify them, there is no reason that this person should suffer any more guilt, anxiety, or unrest about them than a person does whose activity is exclusively heterosexual.

The fact that societal pressures are the chief source of emotional problems related to homosexuality was accepted by none other than neurologist Sigmund Freud, the father of psychoanalysis, many of whose disciples today are in the forefront of the psychiatric clique that insists homosexuality is an illness. Dr. Freud in 1935 wrote: "Homosexuality is assuredly no advantage, but it is nothing to be ashamed of; no vice, no degradation, it cannot be classified as an illness; we consider it to be a variation of the sexual function . . ."

Of course, to say that homosexuality need not be problematic is not to render it universally nonproblematic. The fact is, many people do *not* accept their homosexual desires. If they act on them, they may feel guilty about it. If they refrain from acting, they may feel frustrated — and may still feel guilty, simply about having the desires. If they don't feel guilty about what they do or desire, they may feel a variety of other frustrations: the feeling that many of the good things in life will forever elude them, the fear that they will embarrass family or friends because of their behavior. In Chapter Twenty we identified factors most likely to lead to potency problems among homosexually active men and orgasm problems among homosexually active women. We identified other factors least likely to lead to such problems. Actually, many of these very same factors have precisely the same effect with regard to emotional problems about homosexuality.

Among factors likely to encourage emotional turmoil in the homosexually active or the merely homosexually desirous are:

• Subscribing to a philosophy or being affiliated with a religious organization that regards homosexual activity as immoral, impermissible, or shameful;

• Being in a career where revelation of one's homosexual activity could be damaging;

• Being married to a spouse who does not know about one's homosexual orientation and would not accept the situation;

• Having children, parents, siblings, other family members, and/or longstanding personal acquaintances who would be appalled to learn of one's homosexual orientation;

• Living near these people, especially in a small town that is quite distant from any city having a large homosexually active population;

• Not having opportunities for homosexual relationships, whether for reasons of geography, anatomy, or personality.

If one is accepting of homosexual desire and has the opportunity to gratify it in a guilt-free environment, preferably in relationships characterized by deep emotional commitment or at least affection, the likelihood of being deeply troubled about one's orientation is reduced considerably, if not actually eliminated.

CHAPTER 23

Going Straight

While homosexual desire and/or activity need not be emotionally troublesome, there are some men and women who find it so and would like to pursue heterosexual relationships exclusively. This is certainly possible, though some people find it more difficult to change their orientation than others. Interestingly, while behavioral scientists disagree vehemently about the causes of homosexual desire and the best ways to deal with it, they are in more or less general agreement about the types of people who are most likely to succeed in changing their orientation. The most promising candidates are:

(a) Young; in fact, the younger the better. Once a person has developed long-standing patterns of homosexual behavior, change is much more difficult.

(b) Relatively inexperienced homosexually. The more experience one has and the more satisfying one has found that experience, the less one is likely to be able to make the change.

(c) Experienced heterosexually, especially if the experiences are regarded as "good."

(d) Attractive to the opposite sex, whether by reason of physical attributes, cultural background, money, intelligence, education, wit, kindness, charm, political power, or, better still, all of the above.

Approaches to Altering Homosexual Appetite ———

Behavioral scientists employ a variety of approaches to alter sexual appetite and/or to induce clients to change their patterns of behavior. Here are the principal ones:

BEHAVIOR THERAPY

In its strictest form, this technique seeks to change behavior by rewarding desired activity (or reactions) and punishing that which is undesired. A derivative form, called "aversion therapy," concentrates on punishing the undesired without rewarding the desired.

With respect to homosexual behavior or desires, a strict behavioral therapist might show a male client slides of nude or seminude men and women. When the men appear on the screen, the client is given an electric shock. When the women appear, the shock stops. The slides of men might be made more "undesirable" by having disturbingly loud sounds broadcast into the room while the pictures are on the screen; the slides of women might be made more "desirable" by having pleasant music played while they are on.

In one well-known behavioral experiment in Canada, researchers gave twenty-five homosexually active men an injection of certain drugs that induce nausea and vomiting. Then slides of nude men were shown. After the subjects had recovered from the vomiting, they were given an injection of testosterone, the male hormone, and shown slides of women. After repeating the procedure ten times, the researchers were able to report that six of the twenty-five men had become heterosexually active.

Behavior therapy is hardly anyone's idea of fun (except, perhaps, for a sadistic experimenter). However, it often works for curing such habits as smoking or drinking, and it may sometimes woo (or intimidate) people away from homosexual activity.

COGNITIVE-BEHAVIORAL SITUATION MANIPULATION

This approach, which is favored by Paul Gillette, deviates sharply from the strict behavioral approach but is based on the same fundamental hypothesis that we react to the circumstances in our environment, repeating behavior that we have found rewarding and discontinuing that which we find unrewarding. Cognitive-behaviorists seek to manipulate the environment in such a way that desired behavior is rewarded (and ideally is its own reward) while undesired behavior is punished (and ideally is its own punishment).

In terms of this approach, supported by the studies of Dr. Kinsey and colleagues at the Indiana University Institute for Sex Research and by Masters and Johnson, three factors influence sexual appetite: (1) societal conditioning, (2) availability of partners, and (3) character of experience to date.

In other words, oversimplifying the matter considerably, if you are male and grew up in an environment where relationships with girls were regarded as "dirty," sinful, shameful, or disgusting, and if there were not many attractive and willing girls available with whom to carry out guilt-free experimentation, and if the few experiences you did have with girls were unpleasant (guilt-laden, fearful, clandestine, perhaps characterized by much resistance on the girl's part and partial impotence — or, in any case, great anxiety — on yours), chances are your heterosexual appetites would be dulled and, over a period of years, perhaps extinguished. If at the same time you had homosexual relationships that proved rewarding or even simply less troublesome, you'd be reinforced in your acceptance of them and would probably develop a preference for homosexual activity.

Conversely, if you grew up in an atmosphere where homosexuality was roundly condemned and perhaps even ridiculed, and if the males whom you found attractive rebuffed your expressions of sexual interest, and if the few experiences you did have with men were unpleasant (guilt-laden, fearful, clandestine, perhaps even revealed later by your partner to others of your peers, who scorned you because of it), chances are your homosexual appetites would be dulled and, over a period of years, perhaps extinguished. If at the same time you had heterosexual relationships that proved rewarding or even simply less troublesome, you'd be reinforced in your acceptance of them and would probably develop a preference for heterosexual activity.

Some people, unfortunately, suffer the worst of both worlds, getting discouragement and meeting with frustration both heterosexually and homosexually. Still, the two sides of the balance are rarely if ever perfectly equal: almost inevitably there is greater pleasure (or at least less discomfort) on one side than on the other. This is not to say that we are entirely the victims of our environment, lacking the ability to make choices and influence the stimuli to which we respond. It is only to say that, minus our own efforts to assert control over our environment, our environment may very well assert control over us.

The key, therefore, to the cognitive-behavioral approach to changing sexual orientation — as to just about every other emotional problem — is for a person to work actively at structuring his or her environment in a way that is most apt to produce the desired results. This means if you are homosexually oriented and would prefer not to be, you should attempt to expose yourself to women under circumstances most likely to lead to sexual desire. First, pursue relationships that are not specifically sexual: get to like women as *friends*, get to enjoy their company and have strong feelings of affection for them. At the same time, work at depropagandizing yourself of all conceivable antiheterosexual influences. Question your philosophies, challenge the opinions of people from whom you feel social pressure. If, for example, you were brought up to condemn "impure thoughts" and "unchaste deeds," ask yourself what the basis is for these proscriptions. Refuse to accept a view of life that you deem illogical. Read books by authors who argue against these philosophies. Talk with people who disagree with them. Try to identify specific situations that are heterosexually inhibiting and, insofar as is possible, remove yourself physically from them. In short, do everything you can to make your environment encourage you to have personal relationships with women. Then do whatever you can to make these relationships as pleasant and anxiety-free as possible.

All this is, of course, easier said than done. What isn't? But it *can* be done. When it is, what remains is to pursue sexual relations with those women you find appealing. A number of satisfying heterosexual relationships can lead to development of, if not an actual heterosexual preference, at least the ability to *enjoy* sex with women — either while continuing to have homosexual relationships or while deliberately abstaining from homosexual activity.

RATIONAL-EMOTIVE PSYCHOTHERAPY
This method, a cognitive-behavioral variation, is based on the assumption that people engage in homosexual activity because

they subscribe to illogical beliefs. Writes psychologist Albert Ellis, developer of the technique: "The homosexual's abnormality is not that he wants sex relations with members of his own sex but that he erroneously believes that he must have such relations, and those primarily or even exclusively. It is this irrational premise of his which is his sickness. . . . He is cured, therefore, not if he never has any homosexual desires for the rest of his life, but if he is easily able to handle those that he does have, refuses to give in to them compulsively, and keeps them within the bounds of a generally well-ordered sex life that would also include his having the desire for heterosexual participations."

This is accomplished by persuading the client to share the rational-emotive practitioner's values on the subject and instructing him in ways to change the attitudes that are believed to underlie his behavior.

HORMONE THERAPY

The theory is that the homosexually active male is deficient in certain hormones, notably testosterone. The technique involves injections of the hormone. The results are not definitive. Several studies suggest that sexual focus remains the same, only the strength of the sexual urge changes.

PSYCHOANALYSIS AND OTHER PSYCHOANALYTICALLY ORIENTED APPROACHES

The theory is that people go through four stages of sexual development between infancy and adulthood. Homosexuality is seen as developmental arrest in the third stage. By one means or another, psychoanalytically oriented practitioners attempt to convince patients of the reasonableness of the psychoanalytic explanation. The assumption is that once the explanation is understood and the patient's past examined for factors deemed responsible for the developmental arrest, the responsible factors will eventually be identified and development will automatically resume. Results with this technique are widely regarded as highly unsatisfactory — although the psychoanalytic approach in some instances appears to influence the desired change in orientation.

GROUP "THERAPIES"

The basic technique involves discussion by a group of people about their problems. Members of the group, under the supervision of a practitioner generally known as the "group leader," try to illuminate the problems of other members and offer suggestions on how to understand and cope with them. We are unaware of anyone who overcame homosexual desire as a result of such exposure, although the group approaches may encourage heterosexual development when other factors in a person's environment are conducive to such development.

CHAPTER 24

Transsexualism

Joan entered the physician's office, her face all smiles. She walked over to his desk and displayed her large, light-colored mink coat. "Doctor," she said, "I've been a woman for only sixteen months and look at what my boyfriend gave me. I know women who have been women for forty years and never got a mink."

The physician was particularly impressed because he remembered when Joan was a man: fat, sloppy, and singularly unattractive. This was just before the operation that surgically changed his gender.

After the operation the newly created Joan developed a severe infection of the skin of the lower abdomen. It was cured only after extensive antibiotic therapy. Subsequently she developed a stricture that completely blocked her urinary passageway. It had to be opened surgically, and now she requires monthly urethral dilatations to prevent the canal from closing again. All this notwithstanding, she is delighted with her decision to become a woman. In her new role, she is the complete opposite of her previous self. She is thin, carefully manicured, immaculately groomed. She wears the most fashionable clothing and enjoys knitting and sewing. She has said to the physician on a number of occasions, "I told you I was a woman in a man's body, and I was determined to correct that mistake."

There is no such thing as a woman in a man's body. This figure of speech, which all too many people take literally, is encouraged by the semantic concept of a "mind" or "soul" being a distinct entity that is somehow housed in a person while not being part of the person's body. Actually, "mind" is a substantive for certain processes of the brain: thinking, emoting, judging, perceiving, willing. There is no question that the brain is part of the body. "Soul" is a religious concept of a nonmaterial entity that is everlasting; it has nothing to do with the brain. In any case, neither "mind" nor "soul" has gender. Gender is a classification (root word: the Latin *genus*) based on the structure of one's genitals.

Some people, as it happens, are not happy about the structure of their genitals. They would prefer the configuration of the opposite gender. Behavioral scientists unable to resist the temptation to label people according to shared traits call such persons "transsexuals."

There is another group of people who do not necessarily prefer to be members of the opposite gender but who nonetheless take pleasure, and often obtain sexual arousal and satisfaction, from wearing clothing associated with the opposite gender. Behavioral scientists label them "transvestites."

Transsexualism is a complicated matter. First and most obviously, the procedure involves not merely putting on clothing but drastically restructuring one's body. Second, the decision to undertake this restructuring may be dictated by physical as well as emotional concerns.

For instance, the original "sex change" operation was really an attempt not at change but at definition. The infants and children on whom the operation was performed were not anatomic males or females who wanted to become members of the opposite gender; rather, their sexuality was literally confused. In some cases, biological males were born with undeveloped or underdeveloped genitals. They were identified erroneously at birth as females and were raised by their families as females. When the error of identification was discovered, generally at puberty, hormone treatments and surgery were undertaken to "bring out" the true gender.

In other cases, the patient was a female born with overdeveloped genitals and erroneously identified as male. The reverse of the above procedures was employed to create a clearly female appearance. In still other cases — extremely rare — a baby might be born a hermaphrodite, that is, possessing both male and female genital structures. Hormone therapy and surgery would be undertaken to eliminate one set of structures.

The cause of these defects was a hormone imbalance during the development of the embryo. Normally the developing embryo is exposed to only one type of sex hormone, and this determines the appearance of the sex organs of the newborn. But in certain cases, the hormonal exposure may be mixed or confused due to abnormal developmental processes. The resulting child's external genitals (clitoris, vulva, penis, testicles) may differ from the internal genitals (prostate gland, uterus, ovaries, fallopian tubes). The most common such abnormality is the adrenogenital syndrome, apparently caused by oversecretion from greatly enlarged adrenal glands.

Note well: The purpose of surgery in these cases is not to *change* the patient's gender but to help *define* it. In some cases, the patient possesses the internal organs and hormone activity of one gender while having — or seeming to have — the external structures of the opposite gender. In other cases, there may be internal or external structures of both genders. There is a world of difference between problems of this type and those involving people who are clearly anatomic males or females and who, for whatever reason, desire to change their gender.

The first cases of deliberate gender *change* involved people, generally male, in extraordinary circumstances. For example, in a case reported by *Modern Medicine,* a pediatrician irreparably burned the penis of a newborn boy whom he was attempting to circumcise with an electric cautery device. One choice for the parents was to raise the child as a boy without a functioning penis: he would possess only the tiniest protrusion through which he could urinate but he would almost certainly be incapable of perceiving sexual sensation. Another choice was to have the child undergo surgery and hormone therapy. The surgery would remove what remained of the penis and scrotum and construct in their place a vagina that would to all outward appearances be indistinguishable from that of someone born female. The hormone treatments would ensure development during puberty of female secondary sex characteristics: voice, breasts, body hair. The internal genitals would remain male;

thus, the patient could never give birth. But in every other respect, she would be (or at least seem) female. Deciding that the child's chances for happiness would be much greater under the latter circumstances, the parents opted for sex change.

In other cases, parents have deliberately raised anatomically perfect children as members of the opposite gender. They did so, they said, because they had desperately wanted a child of that gender or for such reasons as believing that they had been visited by some supernatural being who told them to do it. The child would be given the name of a person of the opposite gender, would be made to dress as the opposite gender, and would be reared in every way as if a member of that gender. Often it was not until late childhood or early adolescence that the child, comparing genitals with friends, discovered her or his true gender. Often this led to protracted periods of intense emotional turmoil as the person tried to reorient herself or himself to the "new" gender. In certain cases of this type, sex change surgery and hormone therapy were undertaken in the belief that the person would be less troubled about converting to the gender in which she or he had been raised.

From here, it was a relatively short step to elective transsexual therapy, performed virtually on request. Actually, very few institutions will undertake the treatments simply because someone *wishes* to change gender. But just about anyone who complains of a serious gender problem can find someone to provide the therapy. In a majority of cases, the patient is a man, but there are gender-change programs also for women.

What does treatment entail? In most programs, the first phase is a series of interviews exploring the person's reasons for wanting to change and discussing the feasibility of an operation. For instance, someone with a serious heart condition might not be able to withstand the surgery, or a man with an exceptionally large skeleton might have great difficulty passing as a woman. Legal complications must be considered: married persons, for example, have the problems of divorce and how to provide for their families. If program directors believe that a candidate is acting capriciously or for whatever reason will not benefit from the procedure, they usually refuse to proceed.

Most clinics and independent practitioners discourage the whimsical, the capricious, and the less-than-highly-motivated by charging a steep fee — even for the initial interviews. For example, at the Gender Dysphoria Clinic at Stanford University, Palo Alto, California — one of the most active of an estimated forty gender-change clinics in the United States — the interviews cost $210, even if the clinic ultimately refuses to admit a person. After admission, costs skyrocket. Hospital and surgeons' fees are $4,000, paid in advance. General medical visits, usually for hormone therapy, are $20 each; there may be over a hundred of them during the course of the program. One of the bigger expenses for men is electrolysis, to remove body hair. It usually requires two hundred sessions at $20 each. All told, the full treatment may cost $10,000. (Fortunately, a new depilatory procedure is simpler and less costly. Each hair is taken into a tweezer-like device called a "depilatron." An electric current is run through the hair, and the root is destroyed.)

After the initial interviews, hormone therapy begins. Men receive estrogen, the female hormone, which softens the skin and redistributes the body's fat into the usual female pattern (broader at the hips, flatter at the waist). Women receive androgen, the male hormone, which causes menstruation to stop and produces the usual male secondary sex characteristics: deeper voice, heavier and darker facial and body hair.

The hormone therapy phase generally lasts at least a year and a half. Men are impotent during this time, although women can usually achieve orgasm through clitoral stimulation. The hormones start producing changes after about three months. Now, in most programs, patients are told to begin dressing and living as members of the opposite gender. During this period, they get the opportunity to assess people's reactions to them — and their own reactions — and decide whether they really want to go ahead with the surgery. At Stanford, reports clinic coordinator Marti Norberg, only one in four who begin the program ultimately have the surgery. However, some drop out for monetary reasons and reportedly get treatment from private practitioners at lower fees.

Surgery for men involves two procedures, performed as part of the same operation. In the first procedure, the penis is amputated at the point where it passes under the pubic bone and the testicles are removed. In the second procedure, the skin of the scrotum and surrounding area is fashioned into a pouch that will act as a vagina. The pouch is developed surgically just above the rectum, in the area from which the penis was removed. It is extended inward as deeply as possible. Other female organs, the inner and outer genital lips, are also fashioned from the skin of the area. In some cases, a surgeon will turn the penis "inside out" — that is, will push the outer surface inside, as one might with the finger of a glove — to form the vagina.

The female operation is considerably more complex and is performed in stages. First, a double mastectomy (removal of both breasts) is performed. This generally happens during the eighteen-month transvestite period so that the woman can both adjust to being accepted visually as a man and also develop some sense of what it will be like to *be* a man when the operation is completed. Next, a hysterectomy is performed. Then, in a third operation, an artificial penis and scrotum are fashioned from skin taken from other parts of the body. A silicone implant can keep the penis permanently erect. A new technique, still in the experimental stage, involves a more sophisticated implant that can be filled with liquid or emptied, thus producing erection on demand.

Not surprisingly, gender change has aroused considerable controversy both inside and outside the medical profession. Some physicians condemn it as an unwarranted destruction of undamaged human tissue. Others maintain that the emotional benefits justify the relatively small medical risks. Whatever one's position on the ethics or morality of performing or undergoing the procedure, the medical risks should not be underestimated.

Problems are more prevalent and serious for the male than for the female, owing to limitations of the male anatomy and the character of the surgical procedures.

There are men who do not have sufficient room within the pelvis to permit construction of a functional vagina. The reason for this is that the male pelvis is narrow and sharply angulated, rather like a triangle with the point faced downward, whereas the female pelvis is wide and closer to rectangular in shape, permitting the head of a newborn child to pass under the bones that produce the lowermost arch. The surgically constructed vagina may therefore prove too narrow to accommodate a penis. It may also prove too short. In some patients, a penis can be accommodated in one position that permits the pelvis to be tilted upward at a certain angle, but not in any other. Obviously, careful evaluation of the size of the pelvis should be undertaken before surgery is performed. Most clinics, especially those associated with prestigious teaching hospitals like Stanford, will be scrupulous about this. However, some may not be — and the patient will undergo the operation only to learn afterwards that the anticipated sexual ability of a woman never was achieved.

Whatever the size of the pelvis, a surgically constructed vagina tends to "heal" closed, as does any surgical wound. The patient must each day for the rest of her life dilate the opening and the entire length of the canal, or it will promptly become nonfunctional. Sometimes even with daily stretching the canal closes.

Surgery to reopen the channel can lead to severe complications. An ever-present danger is penetrating the rectum, causing a fistula. If repeated surgery is necessary, emotional problems often develop. The patient may feel that somehow the entire procedure has been a failure — this one thing on which so many hopes were based has gone awry, she was a "failure" as a man and now is a "failure" as a woman.

The surgically built vagina produces no natural secretions. In very rare cases, a newly formed vagina will remain soft and pliable. Much more often, medications must be used daily to keep the walls from drying out and becoming hardened, like the surface of a scab.

Of course, transsexual females can bear no children. This may seem rather obvious, considering that all surgery is external. Yet, some men, poorly informed about biology, seek transsexual surgery expecting that they will be fertile afterwards. Some, having been advised that this is impossible, go ahead with the operation but are dissatisfied, complaining of a sense of incompleteness and inadequacy.

When the surgery is performed, some male organs — the

prostate gland, seminal vesicles, and a portion of the vasa deferentia — are left inside the body. These can create medical problems. When the prostate becomes infected, the woman develops a high fever. If she consults a physician who does not know her original sex, her condition is extremely difficult to diagnose, for there is no reason to suspect infection in that particular site.

Sometimes, if urinary difficulties develop along with the fever, the woman will be referred to a gynecologist. A Foley catheter is inserted into the patient's urethra, and she becomes severely ill. The gynecologist followed the accepted procedure for treating urinary infection in women, who have a very short urethra. But the person who has been transformed from male to female still has a very long, typically masculine urethra. The catheter, placed into an infected area, aggravates the condition. If the gynecologist learns that the patient was once a man, the course of therapy can be changed, the catheter removed, antibiotics given, and surgery performed, if needed. But many transformed women do not want the gynecologist to know — indeed, they take pride in "fooling" the gynecologist — and they do not realize that by withholding the truth they are responsible for their worsening condition.

The prostate can develop benign or cancerous tumors. Indeed, a tumor will develop in about a third of all men over fifty and three-fourths of all over seventy-five. We do not know of any transformed male who has developed either tumor, but with sufficient time and increasing numbers undergoing transsexual surgery the conditions are quite likely to develop. If the patient's original gender is not known, diagnosis will be extremely difficult and can delay treatment beyond a point when the patient's life can be saved. Even if the patient's original gender is known, prostatic surgery in a transformed male would be more complicated than in an original male and might very easily lead to immediate or postoperative complications involving the surgically constructed vagina. A much less serious matter related to the prostate: this is the organ that produces the secretions that a man ejaculates at orgasm. Sometimes a transformed male will continue to ejaculate some material at orgasm.

Still other problems arise with the transformed male's urethra.

Any urethra is very sensitive to trauma and surgery. When you cut across it or injure it in any way, a scar forms at the point of damage. This scar continues to contract and heal, narrowing the passageway and eventually blocking the flow of urine. Because transsexual surgery involves amputation of the penis, the urethra must be cut completely across. This area almost always develops severe scarring and becomes tightly closed. Patients require repeated weekly stretching of the stricture with progressively larger instruments called sounds, and at times require reconstructive surgery to open the urethra. At times reconstructive surgery will provide relief for a few months, then the stricture will reform. Weekly dilatations seem to be the best method of keeping the passage open. Note, of course, that this is in addition to the daily dilatations needed by the surgically constructed vagina.

When the penis is amputated, the point of amputation is just below the pubic bone. Because not all humans have the same anatomy, this point in some patients will not be deep enough inside the body to cut the urethra at a point where it aims the urine downward. As a result, some transformed males cannot sit to void. This creates serious emotional problems for many because they identify sitting to urinate as a confirmation of their femininity — if they must stand, they are still somewhat "masculine." Further surgery can resituate the urethra to aim downward, but each additional surgical procedure brings on additional medical risks.

Though the transformed male has external genitals that appear female, the chromosomal pattern is still male and many secondary sex characteristics remain undisguisedly male. Castration does not, as legend has it, make everyone a soprano; usually the transformed male manages to sound female only by speaking deliberately in a high pitch. Silicone implants may create the appearance of female breasts and male-pattern hair may be removed, but the "Adam's apple" remains masculine-looking. The hips remain their original width, of course, and the hands remain their original size. The hands are a particular source of frustration, for male hands are usually quite a bit larger than those of females. Patients want delicate, "feminine" hands and often are taken aback when a new acquaintance comments that the patient's hands are unusually large.

Some physical traits identified as feminine, like distribution of body fat or softness of the skin, are enhanced by hormone treatments. But subjecting the male body to large doses of these unfamiliar chemicals can create serious medical problems. While results are difficult to evaluate because of the relatively small sample of transformed men on whom to gather data, there are reports of breast cancer in two patients using estrogen and there seems to be an increase in thrombophlebitis in others.

Women who are surgically and hormonally transformed into men have comparable troubles. It is impossible — and probably will remain so for many years — to construct a functioning penis surgically. While a penis-like extension can indeed be created, it does not possess the erectile structures of a natural penis. Plastic splints can create a semblance of erection, but it is clearly not the real thing. An artificial extension of the female urethra permits urination through the surgically-constructed penis. But there have been cases where the plastic tubing used for the construction came apart or separated from the natural urethra.

Hormone treatments hold the same potential for complications in the transformed female as in the transformed male, and there is risk of infection at the point where the surgically constructed penis is joined to what used to be the vaginal lips. Dissatisfactions about not being "completely" male are also reported. Just as the transformed male may be unhappy about large hands and an "Adam's apple," the transformed female may complain of her diminutive physique, small hands, etc. The transformed female cannot ejaculate at orgasm and, of course, cannot sire a child.

Perhaps an even greater number of problems among transformed females would be reported if the operation were more widely performed. One potentially grave threat is cancer related to treatment with male hormones. A definite link has not been established.

Emotional problems, of course, can arise for both genders — and frequently do. Many transformed men and women are distressed to learn that, though they have taken the step that supposedly would make them happy, they still have many of the same problems they had before. One physician is aware of three of his patients, all transformed males, who committed suicide. There may be others of whom he is not aware.

At the Stanford Gender Dysphoria Clinic, of 160 patients transformed as of this writing, three wanted the operation reversed. All three were originally men. One of these said she/he had a religious revelation directing return to a "natural state." Another was dissatisfied because as a woman she could not find work that paid as well as when she had been a man. The third simply felt that her social life had suffered. The operation has never been reversed, and so these women had to keep their surgically created female bodies and content themselves with dressing as men.

Some transformed men and women suffer emotional problems growing out of what might be termed the "vine-covered cottage syndrome." That is, the person feels that a gender change will lead magically to a marriage with the ideal mate and an idyllic life forever after in a dream house by a babbling brook. Unfortunately, this rarely happens. Usually people do not undertake a sex change operation until they are at least thirty and often not until their forties, fifties, or in a few cases even over sixty. If they expect the kind of love life they had in their fantasies as adolescents — as many do — they are sorely disappointed. Finding a perfect mate at forty or fifty is difficult enough for an unaltered man or woman. Finding one after surgical transformation is clearly more difficult. Often, transformed people are avoided by both the homosexually active and the heterosexually active. The former do not want a person of the opposite sex, even if only recently arrived thereat, and the latter are put off by the inconsistent secondary sex characteristics ("Adam's apple," large hands, etc.).

Even if attracting a mate is no problem, difficulties often arise. Among one physician's patients who underwent transformation, one married a man who could not support her. She eventually obtained a divorce. Her second marriage was more successful until her husband lost his job and she had to support him. This marriage also ended in divorce. Of course, that sort of thing happens also in relationships among men and women who never changed their gender. But among those who have, it appears more likely to precipitate severe emotional disturbance — because the person was more desperate to succeed in her or his "new" gender.

All of this having been said, we should add that a great many transformed men and women report great happiness as a result of their transformation. One physician noted the following developments among his own patients, all transformed males:

• One said she was getting married and was so happy about it that she intended to avoid contact with anyone who knew she was once a male. This conversation took place two years after her surgery.

• Another took a job as a secretary and seven months later reported that she had just married her boss.

• Another came to the office with a photo of herself modeling in a national magazine.

• Two patients said that they felt great relief from the problems of homosexuality. One said that she really could not stand "fags" and now she could have sexual relations with a "real man" and it felt wonderful.

Patients who have undergone this surgery are often relieved of pressures from friends and peers to behave heterosexually. "Thank God," said one, "that I no longer have people asking me why I don't find a nice girl to marry. Now I'm the nice girl for someone else to find."

Interestingly, a number of patients became prostitutes. Their success in this profession certainly suggests that their transformation was good enough to warrant their being accepted as female by many men. One of these patients caught syphilis — much to her amazement and, in a sense, to her delight.

One patient was living in a homosexual relationship with another man. When they learned about transsexual surgery, they decided to have the patient undergo it. They jointly paid for the operation. Afterward, they were legally married and have continued this relationship for four years.

Another patient met a South American diplomat and has been dating him steadily for months. He is unaware that she was once a male, even though he reports considerable experience with women.

Still another patient told a boyfriend that he had made her

pregnant. She was convincing enough that he gave her money for an abortion.

One physician routinely asked some transformed patients if they would permit him to interview their parents. Most obligingly arranged a meeting. The parents ranged from unemployed manual laborers to highly educated executives. In each case, they completely accepted the sex change. This fortified the physician's impression that they wanted a girl from the start and encouraged rather than merely tolerated the operation.

One mother said that she noticed that her son was "very feminine" even as a small child. She took him to a number of physicians to see if he could be made "more of a man." Another child had received therapy with male hormones because his penis and testicles were very small. Many parents were less specific about what was "wrong," but they sensed that something was and they could not figure out how to make their child either "more male" or "more female."

This group of patients offers research opportunities that are unique — the opportunity, for example, to investigate what degree of sexual satisfaction is purely physical and what is emotional. The vagina of a transformed male contains no nerve endings. Thus, there is no feeling — the woman is not even aware, on the basis of tactile clues inside the vagina, that she is having sexual relations. Yet many report orgasm. Since none has a clitoris — the organ which contains most sexually sensitive nerve endings in people born female — the question naturally arises, how is orgasm stimulated? Perhaps the phenomenon is — at least under circumstances such as these — purely emotional. Or perhaps destruction of the usual sexually sensitive nerve endings (in men, those of the glans of the penis) leads to development of sexual sensitivity in other nerve endings of the genitopelvic region, especially those of the perineum and pubic mound.

Another interesting question for researchers: men who have been transformed into women are physically capable of continuing coitus indefinitely with no apparent ill effects. What value, if any, does this virtually unlimited sexual capacity have for a partner? Does such capacity aid a relationship or hurt it? In either case, to what extent?

Our overall impression is that most transformed males are happy to be women. They state almost without exception that they have a wonderful sex life — this knowing full well that we know they have no vaginal sensation. In nonsexual matters they seem neither more nor less content than patients who have not undergone gender change.

The husbands of these women said without exception that they were happy with the sexual relationship. The women apparently were able to adjust their sexual "giving" and demands to the wishes of the mate. This makes sense. The woman's own wants being essentially unaffected by penile-vaginal contact, she was able to devote herself completely to the mate's wants — and was both proud of and delighted with her ability to satisfy him. Among fifteen patients who were legally married or privately committed to one relationship, no sexual difficulties were reported. Complaints by the female were limited to such concerns as financial support, conflict with relatives, or problems involving the wife and children of a previous marriage.

APPENDICES

We have done our best to provide accurate information about the organizations listed in the following appendices. Because of the transient nature of many of these groups, however, some errors were unavoidable, between the time of the book's preparation and its publication.

A useful source of the most up-to-date information on gay organizations is Gayellow Pages, revised annually, which lists groups of all kinds across the United States. This publication can be purchased in gay bookstores or by writing Renaissance House, Box 292, Village Station, New York, New York 10014. Gayellow Pages can also be found in the reference departments of some public libraries.

Gay Health Clinics

Several metropolitan areas have health clinics aimed exclusively at homosexually active people. They provide V.D. screening and treatment and usually other health services, especially those relating to sexual activity. Generally they are funded by informally organized coalitions within the gay community and are staffed by volunteer physicians and laymen. Usually treatment is free. Telephone for information about services and hours of operation; some clinics operate only in the evening or on certain days.

CALIFORNIA ————————————————————————————
Los Angeles
Feminist Women's Health Center, 746 Crenshaw Blvd., 90005. (213) 936–7219
Gay Community Services Center, 1213 N. Highland Ave., 90038. (213) 464–7485
San Francisco
Golden Gate Gay Liberation House / Page Street Survival House, 934 Page St., 94117. (415) 431–7688
Helping Hands Gay Community Center, 225 Turk St., 94102.
San Francisco City Clinic, 250 Fourth St., 94103. (415) 558–3804

DISTRICT OF COLUMBIA ———————————————————————
Gay Men's V.D. Clinic, 1556 Wisconsin Ave., N.W., 20007. (202) 965–5476

ILLINOIS ————————————————————————————————
Chicago
Chicago Women's Liberation Union, 2748 N. Lincoln Ave., 60614.
Emma Goldman Women's Clinic, 1317 W. Loyola Ave., 60626. (312) 262–8870
Howard Brown Memorial V.D. Clinic, La Plaza Medical Center, 1250 W. Belden St., 60690. (312) 871–1303, 871–0839

MARYLAND ――――――――――――――――――――――――――
Baltimore
People's Free Medical Clinic, 3028 Greenmount Ave., 21218.

MASSACHUSETTS ―――――――――――――――――――――――
Boston
Fenway Community Health Center, 16 Haviland St., 02115. (617) 267–
7573.
Homophile Community Health Services, 80 Boylston St., Room 855,
02116. (617) 542–5188
Project Place, 32 Rutland St., 02118. (617) 262–3740
New Bedford
New Bedford Women's Health Center, 347 Country St., 02740. (617)
996–3341
Provincetown
Provincetown Drop-in Center, Women's Health Clinic, 14 Center St.,
02657.

MICHIGAN ―――――――――――――――――――――――――――
Detroit
Feminist Women's Health Center, 2445 W. Eight Mile Rd., 48203. (313)
892–7990

NEW YORK ―――――――――――――――――――――――――――
New York City
Gay Men's Health Project, 74 Grove St., Room 2-RW, 10014. (212) 691–
6969

OHIO ――――――――――――――――――――――――――――――
Cincinnati
Cincinnati Free Clinic, 2444 Vine St., 45219. (513) 621–4700
Columbus
Gay Clinic, c/o Open Door Clinic, 237 E. Seventeenth Ave., 43201.

RHODE ISLAND ――――――――――――――――――――――――
Providence
Metropolitan Community Health Services, 290 Westminster St., 02903.
(401) 274–1693

WISCONSIN ————————————————————————————————————

Madison
Gay VD Clinic, Box 687, 53701. (608) 257–7575
Milwaukee
Gay People's Union Examination Center for V.D., Farwell Center, 1568
   N. Farwell Ave., 53202.

APPENDIX B

Gay Organizations

The organizations listed below range from activist groups to community service organizations to gay chapters of Alcoholics Anonymous. Most do not provide health services; however, they generally maintain lists of physicians who are members of the gay community or other physicians who provide hassle-free treatment of sexual problems. Most organizations also have information about free health clinics and about local psychologists, psychiatrists, and other counselors.

ALABAMA
Tuscaloosa
Gaze, Box 5877, University of Alabama, 35486.

ALASKA
Fairbanks
Gay Co-op, Box 81265, 99701. (907) 456–6517

ARIZONA
Phoenix
Gay People's Alliance, Box 21461, 83036. (602) 252–2135
Tempe
Gay Liberation Arizona Desert (GLAD), Box 117, 85281. (602) 252–0713
Gay Women's Liberation, 1414 S. McAllister, 85281. (602) 968–0743

CALIFORNIA
Anaheim
Gay Center, 1120 Santa Ana Blvd., 92802.
Aptos
Lesbian and Gay Men's Union, Student Affairs Office, Cabrillo College, 6500 Soquel Drive, 95003. (408) 426–LIFE
Atascadero
Atascadero Gay Encounter, c/o Gerry Olsen, Drawer A, 93422.

Berkeley
Berkeley Women's Center, 2112 Channing Way, 94704. (415) 548–4343
Gay Students Union, 3rd Floor, Eshleman Hall, University of California, 94720.
June 28th Union, Box 4387, 94704. (415) 654–1578
Men's Center, 2700 Bancroft Way, 94704. (415) 845–4823
The Pacific Center for Human Growth, 2329 San Pablo Ave. (415) 841–6224
Social Action Research, 2728 Surant Ave., 94704.
Claremont
Gay Student Union of the Claremont Colleges, c/o Counseling Center, 735 Dartmouth Ave., 91711. (714) 626–8511, ext. 3038
Costa Mesa
Gay Community Center of Orange County, 215 E. Twenty-third St., 92626. (714) 642–4253
Cotati
Gay Students Union, Sonoma State College, 94928. (707) 795–9950
Culver City
Lesbian Activists, Box 2023, 90230. (213) 837–0557, 392–8780
Davis
Gay Students at U.C. Davis, c/o Student Activities, Memorial Union, 95616. (916) 752–3495
Fresno
Fresno Gay Community Center, 2542 E. Belmont Ave., 93727. (209) 268–2011
Gay People's Union, California State University, 93710. (209) 237–6536
Lesbian & Sexuality Task Force, 420 N. Van Ness Ave., 93701. (209) 233–2384
Fullerton
Gay Students Educational Union, California State University, Student Activities, 92634. (714) 497–1687
Hayward
Gay People's Union of Alameda County, Box 3935, 94540.
Irvine
Gay Students Union of U.C. Irvine, Student Activities Office, 92664. (714) 833–1059
Laguna Beach
Concerned Citizens Group, c/o By-the-Sea Motel, 475 N. Coast Highway, 92651. (714) 494–1608
Kalos Kagathos Foundation, Box 416, 92652. (714) 494–1608
Lesbian Feminists of Orange County, 686 S. Coast Highway, 92651.

Long Beach
Gay Liberation Front, 921 Olive Ave., 90813. (213) 436–7710
Gay Student Union, California State University at Long Beach, 1250
   Bellflower Blvd., 90840.
Los Angeles
Brotherhood of David, 1815½ Veteran Ave., 90025.
Christopher Street West Association, Box 3949, 90028.
Gay Community Services Center, 1213 North Highland Ave., 90038.
   (213) 464–7415
Gay Liberation Front, East L.A. College, 5357 E. Brooklyn Ave., 90022.
Gay Sisterhood, U.C.L.A., Women's Resource Center, 90 Powell Library,
   405 Hilgard Ave., 90024. (213) 825–3945
Gay Students of People's College of Law, 2228 W. Seventh St. 90057.
   (213) 661–5135
Gay Students Union, U.C.L.A., 411 Kerckhoff Hall, 308 Westwood
   Plaza, 90024. (213) 825–8053
Gay Youth, 1614 Wilshire Blvd., 90017. (213) 482–3062
Greater Liberated Chicanos, Box 38216, 90038. (213) 851-0788
Lavender and Red Union, 6844 Sunset Blvd., 90028. (213) 465–9285
Lavender People, c/o Hunter, 507½ Glenrock Ave., 90024.
Lesbian Activist Women, 1213 N. Highland Ave., 90038.
Lesbian Feminists, 1027 S. Crenshaw Blvd., 90015.
One, Inc., 2256 Venice Blvd., 90006. (213) 735–5252
Van Ness Recovery House, 1322 Van Ness N., 90028. (213) 463–4266
Mountain View
Alex & Cal Gay People's Union, 1961 Old Middlefield Way, 94943. (415)
   964–5333
North Hollywood
Women's Rap Group, Metropolitan Community Church in the Valley,
   11717 Victory Blvd.
Redding
Human Awareness, Box 566, 96001. (916) 246–9686
Redlands
Lesbian Rap Group, Y.W.C.A., Olive St., 92373.
Riverside
Gay Students' Union, University of California, c/o Associated Students,
   92507. (714) 787–3621
Riverside Women's Center, 4046 Chestnut St., 92501.
Sacramento
CSUS Gay Liberation, c/o James Graham or Charles Moore, Department
   of English, 6000 J St., 95819. (916) 454–6920
Gay Alcoholics Anonymous, 1617 Twenty-fourth St., 95816.

Gay Counseling and Information Services, 4949 Thirteenth Ave. (916) 441–5116

Gay Students Union, Sacramento City College, Student Activities, 3835 Freeport Blvd., 95822. (916) 422–9313

Gay Youth Encounter Group, Box 15765, 95813. (916) 444–0805

Lesbian Feminist Alliance, c/o A.S.S.C., California State University, 95810.

Sacramento Women's Center, 2220 J St., 95816.

San Diego

Gay Center for Social Services, 2550 B St., 92120. (714) 232–7528

San Francisco

Gay Action, 330 Grove St., 94102. (415) 431–1522

Gay People United, 854 Noe St., #2, 94114. (415) 731–3054

Gay Students at Hastings College of Law, c/o Associated Students, 198 McAllister St., 94102.

Gay Students Coalition, c/o Student Activities, San Francisco City College, 94132. (415) 661–9561

Mattachine Society, 384 Ellis St., 94102. (415) 474–6995

Pride Foundation, Box 1983, 94101. (415) 863–9000

Society for Individual Rights (SIR), 83 Sixth St., 94103. (415) 781–1570

San Jose

Gay Student Union, c/o Student Activities Office, San Jose State University, 95192.

San Mateo

Peninsula Group of Concern, Box 5071, 94402. (415) 573–8027

San Rafael

The Other Side, Box 132, 94902. (415) 456–9981

Santa Barbara

Gay People's Union, Box 15048, University of California at Santa Barbara, 93107. (805) 962–7373

Gay Women's Group, 6504 Pardall Rd., 93102. (805) 968–5774

Santa Cruz

Lesbian & Gay Men's Union, Box 5188, 95063. (408) 426–LIFE

Santa Monica

Lesbian Activists, c/o Women's Center, 237 Hill St., 90405.

The Tide Collective at the Women's Center, 1005-B Ocean Ave. (213) 394–4829

Stanford

Gay People's Union at Stanford, Box 8265, 94305. (415) 497–1488

Stockton

San Joaquin County Gays, Anderson Y Center, University of the Pacific, 95211. (209) 466–1496

Ventura
Ventura County Gay Alliance, c/o Ventura Library, Topping Room, Main St., 93001.

COLORADO ─────────────────────────────────
Boulder
Boulder Gay Coalition, Box 1402, 80302. (303) 492–8567
Boulder Women's Resource Center, 2750 Spruce St. (303) 447–9670
Lesbian Caucus of the Women's Liberation Coalition, University of Colorado, UMC-181, 80302. (303) 492–8910
Denver
Denver Lesbian Center, 1895 Lafayette, 80206. (303) 573–6604
Gay Coalition of Denver Inc., Box 18501, 80218. (303) 831–8838
Gay Students Association, Metropolitan State College, Box 39, 250 W. Fourteenth Ave., 80204. (303) 892–6111
Lesbian Task Force of NOW, 1400 Lafayette, 80218.
Fort Collins
Fort Collins Gay Alliance, Student Center Box 210, Colorado State University, 80521.
Littleton
Lesbian Task Force, c/o Marge Johnson, 5720 South Pearl, 80121.

CONNECTICUT─────────────────────────────────
Bridgeport
Kalos Society/Gay Liberation Front Bridgeport, c/o Daniel M. Levitch, 82 Park Terrace, 06604.
Middletown
Wesleyan Gay Alliance, c/o Wesleyan Women's Center, Wesleyan Station, 06457.
New Haven
Gay Alliance at Yale, 2031 Yale Station, 06520. (203) 436–8945
Gay Women's Group, c/o Women's Liberation Center, Box 3438, Yale Station, 06519. (203) 436–0272, 432–2913
New Haven Women's Liberation Center, Box 3438 Yale Station, 06520. (203) 436–0272
Norwich
E. Conn. G.A., Apt. 2, 37 Otrobando Ave., 06360. (203) 889–7530
Storrs
University of Connecticut Gay Alliance, U-8 University of Connecticut, 06268. (203) 429–1448

DELAWARE ————————————————————————————
Greenville
Delaware Separatists Dyke Group, Box 3526, 19807. (302) 478–1246
Newark
Gay Community of the University of Delaware, Episcopal Student Center, W. Park Place, 19711.

DISTRICT OF COLUMBIA ——————————————————
Gay Activist Alliance/DC, Box 2554, 20013. (202) 331–1418
Gay Youth, 1724 Twentieth St., N.W., 20009. (202) 387–3777
Mattachine Society of Washington, Box 1032, 20013. (202) 363–3881
National Gay Student Center, 2115 S St., N.W., 20008. (202) 265–9890
NOW Task Force on Sexuality, 1424 Sixteenth St., N.W., #104, 20009.
Washington Area Gay Community Council, 1724 205th St., N.W., 20009. (202) 234–4387
Washington Area Women's Center, 2453 Eighteenth St., N.W., 20009.

FLORIDA ——————————————————————————————
Clearwater
Suncoast Gay Community Services, 201 W. Rogers St., 33516. (305) 441–3136
Fort Myers
NOW S & L Task Force, c/o Barbara Kelly, 2229A Stella St., 33901.
Gainesville
Women Unlimited, 115 S. Main St., 32601.
Hollywood
Stonewall Committee, Box 2084, 33020.
Jacksonville
Gay Alliance for Political Action, GAPA, c/o Dr. Rosan, 1035 May St., Apt. 3, 32204. (305) 354–5650
Miami
Alliance for Individual Rights, Inc., Box 330414, 33133.
Dade County N.O.W. — Lesbian Task Force, Box 330265, 33133. (305) 672–5133
Gay Community Services of So. Florida, Box 721, Coconut Grove Station, 33133. (305) 445–3511
University of Miami Gay Alliance, Box 8895 University Branch, Coral Gables, 33124.
Tallahassee
Feminist Women's Health Center, 1017 Thomasville Rd, 32303. (904) 224–9600
Tallahassee Women's Center, Box 6826, Florida State University, 32312.

Tampa
Gay Coalition of the University of South Florida, Center 1466, University of South Florida, 33620.
Lesbian Resource Center, 1208 W. Platt St., 33606.
Tampa Daughters of Bilitis, Rte. 1, Box 110, Lithia, 33547. (813) 689–4074

GEORGIA —————————————————————————————
Athens
Committee on Gay Education, Box 2467, University Station, 30602. (404) 599–4015
Gay Academic Union, c/o Lyndrn Hall, 357 S. Milledge Ave., 30602. (404) 599–4015
Atlanta
Atlanta Lesbian Feminist Alliance, Box 3784, 30309. (404) 523–7786
Libertarians for Gay Rights, 2936 Skyland Drive, 30341.
Southeastern Gay Coalition, Box 7922, 30309.

HAWAII —————————————————————————————
Honolulu
Love & Peace Together, Sexual Identity Center, Box 3224, 96801. (808) 524–4699
Wahiawa
Gay Liberation Hawaii, 95-065 Waikalani Dr. F 205, 96786. (808) 623–4334

IDAHO —————————————————————————————
Moscow
Northwest Gay People's Alliance, attn. Gib Preston, Box 8758, 83843.
Women's Center, University of Idaho, Administration Center Building, #109, 84343.

ILLINOIS —————————————————————————————
Carbondale
Gay Liberation, Southern Illinois University Student Activities, 62901.
Chicago
Advocates of Gay Action, Box 872, 60690. (312) 929–4357
Chicago Lesbian Liberation, c/o Lesbian Feminist Center, 3523 N. Halsted St., 60657.
Chicago Women's Liberation Union, 2748 N. Lincoln Ave., 60614. (312) 953–6808

Circle Campus Gay Liberation, University of Illinois, 750 S. Halsted St., Room 518, Circle Center, 60607. (312) 996–4843.

Daughters of Bilitis, Chicago Area, Box 2043, Melrose Park, 60164.

Gay Caucus of Youth against War and Fascism, Suite 310, 542 S. Dearborn St., 60605. (312) 922–0326.

Gay People's Legal Committee, 913 W. Fullerton Ave., 60614. (312) 750–2590.

Gay Pride Planning Committee, 343 S. Dearborn St., Suite 1719, 60604. (312) 939–4600.

Gay Speakers Bureau, Box 2377, 60690. (312) 348–8243.

Gay Youth, c/o Gay Horizons, Box 1319, 60690.

Lesbian Feminist Center, 3523 N. Halsted St., 60657. (312) 935–4250

One of Chicago, Box 53, 60690. (312) 372–8616

Oscar Wilde's Children Foundation, Inc., Box 872, 60690.

Rogers Park Gay Center, 7109 N. Glenwood Ave. 60626. (312) 262–0537

United Front of Gay Organizations, Box 872, 60690.

Unity, c/o Mary Houlihan, 1221 W. Sherwin Ave., 60626. (312) 262–9609

University of Chicago Gay Liberation, 1212 E. Fifty-ninth St., 60637. (312) 753–3274

De Kalb

Gay Liberation Front, Northern Illinois University, Box 74, Student Activities, 60115. (815) 753–0518

Evanston

Northwestern University Gay Union, Box 60, Norris Center, 1999 Sheridan Rd., 60201. (312) 492–3227

Macomb

Friends, Box 296, 61455.

Melrose Park

Daughters of Bilitis (Chicago area), Box 2043, 60164.

Normal

Gay People's Alliance, 225 N. University Ave., #2-C, 61761. (309) 438–3411

Springfield

Springfield Gay Liberation, c/o Spoon River Co-op, 122 S. Fourth St., 62701. (217) 528–0867, 529–3740, 522–3034

Streamwood

Fox Valley Gay Association, Box 186, 60103. (312) 697–0623, 892–5278

Urbana

Gay Illini, 284 Illini Union, University of Illinois, 61801.

INDIANA ——————————————————————————————————————
Bloomington
Bloomington Gay Alliance, Room 48-E, Indiana Memorial Union, Indiana University, 47401. (812) 332–5785
Mishawaka
Lambda Society of Michiana, Box 881, 46544. (219) 259–2810
Notre Dame
Notre Dame Students Group Gay Alliance, Box 206, 46556.
Richmond
Earlham Gay People's Union, Earlham College, 47374.
South Bend
South Bend Gay Alliance, 1527 Kemble St., 46613. (219) 287–2552
West Lafayette
Purdue Gay Alliance, Box 510, 47907.

IOWA ——————————————————————————————————————
Ames
Lesbian Alliance, 1287 I.S.U. Station, 50010.
Open Line, 2502 Knapp St., 50010.
Des Moines
Gay Community Services Center, 3905 Crocker, 50312.
Grinnell
Grinnell College Gay Community, Grinnell College, c/o Student Affairs Office, 50112.
Iowa City
Gay Liberation Front, University of Iowa, Student Activities Center, 52240. (319) 353–7162
Iowa City Lesbian Alliance, 3 E. Market St., 52240. (319) 353–6265
Midwest Gay Pride Planning Committee, c/o Gay Liberation Front, University of Iowa, Student Activities Center, 52240. (319) 337–7677

KANSAS ——————————————————————————————————————
Emporia
Gay People of Emporia, c/o Student Organizations Office, Memorial Union, Kansas State College, 66801. (316) 342–0641
Lawrence
Lawrence Gay Liberation Front, Room 104B, Kansas Union, University of Kansas, 66045. (913) 842–7505
Wichita
Wichita Gay Community Association, Box 13013, 67213.

KENTUCKY ————————————————————
Louisville
Gay Liberation/Daughters of Bilitis, 416 Belgravia Court, 40208. (502) 635–5841
NOW Task Force on Sexuality & Lesbianism, c/o Carolyn Fopp, 230 Franck Ave., 40206.

LOUISIANA ————————————————————
New Orleans
Daughters of Bilitis, Box 52113, 70152.
Tulane University Gay Students Union, c/o Associated Student Body, University Center, Tulane University, 70118. (504) 865–6208, 865–4735

MAINE————————————————————————
Orono
Wilde-Stein Club, c/o Memorial Union, University of Maine, 04473. (207) 581–2571
Pleasant Point
Maine Gay Indians, c/o Deanna Francis, Passamaquoddy Library, 04667.
Portland
Maine Gay Task Force, Box 4524 DS, 04112.
University of Maine Gay Students Group at Portland-Gorham, c/o Maine Gay Task Force, Box 4524 DS, 04112.
Waterville
The Open Door, Box 901, Roberts Union, Colby College, 04901.

MARYLAND ————————————————————
Baltimore
Baltimore Gay Alliance, Box 13438, 21203. (301) 235–HELP
Baltimore Women's Liberation Movement, 101 E. Twenty-fifth St., Suite B-2, 21218.
Gay Alcoholics Anonymous, c/o First Unitarian Church, 1 W. Hamilton St. 21201.
Gay Women's Community Center, c/o People's Free Medical Clinic, 3028 Greenmount Ave., 21218.
Gay Women's Open House, 3032 Abell Ave., 21218. (301) 366–8990
Lesbian Community Center, 3028 Greenmount Ave., 21218. (301) 235–8593
Lesbian Speakers Bureau, Women's Center, 101 E. Twenty-fifth St., B-2, 21218. (301) 366–6475

College Park
Gay Student Alliance, Student Union Bldg., University of Maryland, 20742. (301) 454–4855
Largo
Gay People's Group of Prince George's Community College, c/o Student Activities Office, 301 Largo Rd., 20870.
Simpsonville
PEER, Box 27, 21150.
Towson
Gay Student Alliance, Box 2244, Towson State College, York Road, 21204.

MASSACHUSETTS ———————————————————————
Amherst
Everywoman's Center, Goodell Hall, University of Massachusetts, 01002. (413) 545–0883
Gay Women's Caucus, University of Massachusetts, 413-C Stanford Union, 01002. (413) 545–3438
Hampshire Gay Friends, c/o Mike Gross, School of Natural Science, Hampshire College, 01002. (413) 545–4882
People's Gay Alliance, R.S.O. 368, Lincoln Campus Center, University of Massachusetts, 01002. (413) 545–0154
Southwest Women's Center, McKinnie House, University of Massachusetts, 01002. (413) 545–0626
Student Homophile League, R.S.O. 368, Lincoln Campus Center, University of Massachusetts, 01002. (413) 545–0154
Boston
Black Gay Men's Caucus, c/o G.C.N., Box 9600, 22 Bromfield St., 02108.
Boston College Homophile Union, Box B28, Chestnut Hill, 02167. (617) 277–8096
Boston Gay Youth, c/o Project Lambda, Charles Street Meeting House, 70 Charles St., 02114.
Boston University Gays, c/o Program Resources Office, 775 Commonwealth Ave., Student Union, 02215. (617) 353–2000
Charles Street Meeting House, 70 Charles St., 02114. (617) 523–0368
Daughters of Bilitis, 419 Boylston St., Room 323, 02116. (617) 262–1592
Emerson Homophile Society, Box 1253, Emerson College Union, 96 Beacon St., 02108. (617) 262–2010
Fengay, c/o Fenway Community Health Center, 16 Haviland St., 02115. (617) 267–1066
Fort Hill Faggots for Freedom, 59 Centre St., Roxbury, 02119. (617) 440–8551, 442–6029

Gay Media Action, c/o Gay Community News, Box 5000, 22 Bromfield St., 02108. (617) 523–1081

Gay People's Group at the University of Massachusetts, c/o Center for Alternatives, Room 620, University of Massachusetts at Columbia Point, 02125. (617) 287–1900, Ext. 2396.

Gay Speakers Bureau, Box 482, West Somerville, 02114. (617) 547–1451

Gay Youth Advocates, c/o Meeting House, 70 Charles St., 02114. (617) 227–8587

Northeastern Gay Students Organization, c/o Student Activities Office, 255 E-11 Center, 360 Huntington Ave., 02115. (617) 253–5440

Otherfund, Inc., Box 1997, 02105.

Project Lambda, Charles Street Meeting House, 70 Charles St., 02114. (617) 227–8587

Cambridge

Cambridgeport Gays, c/o GCN Box 6500, 22 Bromfield St. 02108.

Harvard-Radcliffe Gay Students Association, 198 Memorial Hall, Harvard University, 02138. (617) 498–1927

Lesbian Liberation, c/o Women's Educational Center, Inc., 46 Pleasant St., 02139. (617) 354–8807

MIT Student Homophile League, Massachusetts Institute of Technology, 142 Memorial Drive, Rm. 50-306, 02139. (617) 253–5440

Charlemont

Pioneer Valley Gay Union, c/o Windy Hill, Grace Church, Basement Meeting Room, 01370.

Fitchburg

Homophile Union of Montachusett, Box 262, 01420.

Haverhill

Gaypeople/Drop-in Center, Campus Center, 100 Elliot St., 01830. (617) 374–0929

Leominster

Homophile Union of Montachusett, Box F-5, 01453.

Medford

Tufts Gay Community, c/o Student Activities Office, 02155. (617) 776–0921

North Dartmouth

Southern Massachusetts University Gay Alliance, Campus Center, 02747. (617) 997–9321

Northampton

Valley Women's Center, 200 Main St., 01060. (413) 586–2011

Provincetown

Gay Activists Alliance, c/o Postmaster, General Delivery, 02657. (617) 487–3393

Salem
Gay Task Force of the Human Sexuality Program, Salem State College, 01970.
Springfield
Springfield Gay Alliance, Box 752, 01101. (413) 583–3904
Waltham
Bagel (Brandeis Gays), Box 2089, Brandeis University, 02154.
Waltham-Watertown Gays, c/o Gay Community News, Box 7100, 22 Bromfield St., 02108.
Wellesley
Wellesley College Mytilene Society, c/o Women's Center, Wellesley College, 02181.
Westfield
Sexual Identity Awareness Organization, Westfield State College, Parenzo, Box 197, 01085.
Worcester
Another Way Drop-in Center, 64 Chandler St., 01601. (617) 756–0730.
Clark & Holy Cross Gay People's Alliance, Box A-70, Clark University, 01610.
Worcester Gay Union, Box 359, Federal Station, 01601. (617) 752–8330

MICHIGAN ————————————————————————————————
Allendale
Gay Alliance, Grand Valley State College, 49401.
Ann Arbor
Ann Arbor Lesbian Band, c/o Susan, 533 N. Main St., 48104.
Gay Awareness Women's Kollective, c/o Gay Women's Advocates Office, 326 Michigan Union, University of Michigan, 48104.
Gay Liberation Front, 325 Michigan Union, 530 State St., 48104. (313) 763–4168, 761–2044
Gay Women's Advocates Office, 326 Michigan Union, University of Michigan, 48104.
Male Liberation Collective, Box 1025, 48106.
Bloomfield Hills
Identity Center, Box 710, 48103. (313) 469–3311
Detroit
Committee for Gay Rights, Box 631-A, 48232. (313) 831–1476
Gay Center, 906 W. Forest Ave., 48201.
Gay Speakers Bureau, c/o Gay Liberation Front, Room 169, MacKenzie Hall, Wayne State University, 48202.
One in Detroit, 724 W. McNichols Rd., 48203. (313) 341–1980

Wayne State Gay Liberation Front, Box 23 UCB, WSU, 48202. (313) 577–3450

East Lansing
Ambitious Amazons, Box 811, 48823.
Gay Liberation Movement, 309 Student Services Bldg., Michigan State University, 48823. (313) 353–9797
Gay Nurses Alliance, c/o Ambitious Amazons, Box 811, 48823.
Lambda, Inc., Box 416, 48823.

Grand Rapids
Lesbian Nation, 240 Charles St., 49503. (616) 548–4454, 774–0425
Western Michigan Gay Alliance, 240 Charles St., 49503. (616) 456–7129

Kalamazoo
Lambda of Kalamazoo, Inc., Box 2213, 49003. (616) 344–7629

Mount Clemens
Equadare Society, 36 Ahrens St., 48043.

Mount Pleasant
Central Michigan Gay Liberation, Inc., Box 34, Warriner Hall, Central Michigan University 48859. (517) 774–3822

Rochester
Gay Liberation Front Oakland, c/o Community House, Oakland Center, Oakland University, 48063.

Southfield
Circle Club, Box 1003, Northland Station, 48075. (616) 835–3450

MINNESOTA ———————————————————————————————

Mankato
Mankato Gay Consciousness, Box 58, Centennial Student Union, Mankato State College, 56001. (507) 387–4408

Minneapolis
Gay Community Service, Box 3589, Upper Nicollet Station, 55403. (612) 332–0622
Gay House, Inc., 4419-A Nicollet, 55409. (612) 822-3322
Gay Woman's Rap Group, c/o Gay House, 4419 Nicollet Ave., 55409.
Lesbian Resource Center, 2104 Stevens Ave., South, 55404. (612) 871–2601
Metro Gay Students Union, Metropolitan State Junior College, 50 Willow St., 55403.
Minnesota Gay Activists, B-67CMU, University of Minnesota, 55455.
Minnesota Committee for Gay Rights, Box 4226, St. Anthony Falls Station, 55414. (612) 871–3111

MISSISSIPPI ———
Jackson
Mississippi Gay Alliance, Box 8342, 39204. (601) 353–6447
Mississippi Gay Alliance/Jackson Chapter, Box 8342, 39204.
Mississippi Lesbians, Box 8342, 39204. (601) 355–6935
Gay Counseling & Educational Projects, c/o Mississippi Gay Alliance,
    Box 4470, Mississippi State University, 39762.

MISSOURI ———
Columbia
Gay Liberation Executive Board, Ecumenical Center, 813 Maryland
    Ave., 65201.
Gay Liberation/Columbia, Box 1672, 65201.
Gay Liberation Front, University of Missouri, c/o Lawrence Eggleston,
    1723 W. Worley Ave., Apt. 6-A, 65201.
Missouri Alliance for Gay Rights, Box 1672, 65201.
Joplin
Committee for Gay Justice, c/o Billy Walker, 2319 Kentucky, 64801.
Kansas City
Gay Community House, 3825 Virginia Ave., 64109. (816) 931–3579
Gay People's Union of Kansas City, 3825 Virginia Ave., 64109. (816)
    931–3579
Joint Committee for Gay Rights, 1301 Brush Creek #19, 64110. (816)
    561–9381
Kansas City Women's Liberation Union and Lesbian Alliance, 3621
    Charlotte, 64109. (861) 753–2634
Lesbian Alliance, c/o Kansas City Women's Liberation Union, 3621
    Charlotte, 64109.
St. Louis
Gay People's Alliance, Box 1068, Washington University, 63130.
Lesbian Alliance of St. Louis, Box 4201, 63163.
Mandrake Society of Greater St. Louis, Box 7213, 63177.
Metropolitan Life Services Center, 4746-A McPherson Ave., 63108.
    (314) 367–0447
A Woman's Place: Lesbian Alliance of St. Louis, 3400 Miami, 63118.
    (314) 664–7249, 664–6442
Missoula
Lambda, University of Montana, Sociology Dept., 59801. (406) 728–
    0199

NEBRASKA ——————————————————————————————
Lincoln
Gay Resources Center, 333 No. Fourteenth St., 68508.
University of Nebraska Gay Action Group and Lincoln Gay Action Group, 333 N. Fourteenth St., 65808. (402) 475–5710

NEVADA ————————————————————————————————
Reno
Daughters of Bilitis, Box 5025, 89503.

NEW HAMPSHIRE——————————————————————————
Durham
University of New Hampshire Gay Students Organization, c/o Memorial Union Building, 03824.
Northwood
Occupant, Box 137, 03216.
Portsmouth
Seacoast Area Gay Alliance, Box 1424, 03801.

NEW JERSEY —————————————————————————————
Bradley Beach
Central Jersey Daughters of Bilitis, Box 27, 07720.
Cherry Hill
Gays of South Jersey, c/o Unitarian Church, 401 N. Kings Highway, 08106.
Fanwood
Daughters of Bilitis in New Jersey, Box 62, 07203. (201) 233–3848
Garwood
United Sisters, Box 41, 07027. (201) 233–3848
Hackensack
Gay Teachers Caucus of National Education Association, 32 Bridge St., 07601. (201) 489–2458
Jersey City
Gay Rights of People Everywhere (GROPE), Jersey City State College, c/o S.G.A.C., 2039 Kennedy Blvd., 07305. (201) 432–8815.
Mahwah
Alternative Sexual Life-styles Association, Ramapo College, 07430. (201) 825–2800, Ext. 463
Morristown
Gay Activists Alliance in Morris County, Box 137, Convent Station, 07961. (201) 347–6234
Newark
Rutgers Activists for Gay Education (RAGE), Box 6, 350 High St., 07102.

New Brunswick
New Brunswick Task Force on Gay Liberation, c/o General Delivery, 08901.
Rutgers University Homophile League, R.P.O. 2901, Rutgers University, 08903. (201) 932–7886
Orange
Organization for Gay Awareness, Box 41, 07050.
Princeton
Gay Alliance of Princeton, Princeton University, 08540.
Gay People of Princeton, Box 2303, 08540.
South Hackensack
Gay Activists Alliance of New Jersey, Box 1734, 07606. (201) 343–6402
Union
Gay Coalition, Kean College of New Jersey, Student Activities, Student Center, 07083. (201) 289–4330
Wayne
Gay Activists Alliance, William Paterson College, c/o Student Center, 300 Pompton Road, 07470. (201) 881–2157
Willingboro
Gay South Jersey, 71 Hamilton Lane, 08046. (609) 667–0752
Gay Students at Glassboro, c/o 71 Hamilton Lane, 08046.

NEW MEXICO───────────────────────
Albuquerque
Juniper, Box 4606, 87106. (505) 777–2565
New Mexico Gay People's Union, 3214 Silver S.E., 87106.
San Juan Pueblo
Circle of Loving Companions, Box 8, 87566. (505) 852–4404
Santa Fe
Leathersister, c/o Women's Center, 220 W. Manhattan, 87501.
Women's Center, 220 W. Manhattan, 87501.

NEW YORK ───────────────────────
Albany
Capital District Gay Community Council, Box 131, 12201. (518) 462–6138
Capital District Gay Political Caucus, Box 131, 12201.
Gay Alliance, SUNY Albany, Box 1000 DD, SUNYA Station, 12203. (518) 434–4959
Gay Community House, 332 Hudson Ave., 12210. (518) 462–6138
Lesbians for Liberation, Box 131, 12201.

Alfred
Alfred Gay Liberation, Box 472, 14802. (607) 587–8848
Annandale-on-Hudson
Gay Liberation Front, Bard College, Box 87, 12504.
Binghamton
Binghamton Gay Liberation, Box 2000, Harpur College, State University
 of New York, 13901.
Brockport
Brockport Gay Freedom League, Student Union BSG Office, 14420.
 (716) 395–2462
Buffalo
Gay Community Services Center, 1350 Main St., 14209. (716) 881–5335
Gay Law Students at SUNY Buffalo, O'Brien Hall, North Campus,
 14260.
Gay Liberation Front/SUNYAB, College F (Tolstoy) House, Winspear
 Ave., 14214.
Mattachine Society of the Niagara Frontier, Box 975, Ellicott Station,
 14205.
Sisters of Sappho, Box 975, Ellicott Station, 14205.
Student Alliance for Gay Equality (SAGE), 1300 Elmwood Ave., 14222.
Flushing
Project Help, attn. Pete Martin, 143-29 Franklin Ave., 11353.
New York State Coalition of Gay Organizations, c/o Gay People's Center,
 306 E. State St., 14850.
Fredonia
Homophile Education of Fredonia, State University College Student
 Center, S.G.A. Office, 14063. (716) 672–4128
Garden City
Individual Sexual Freedom Coalition, Nassau Community College,
 Stewart Ave., 11530. (516) 546–2383
Geneseo
Gay Freedom Coalition, Box 38 College Union, State University College,
 14454. (716) 245–5891
Hempstead
Hofstra United Gays, Box 67, Student Center, Hofstra University, 11550.
Herkimer
Gay Liberation, c/o Reckeweg, Herkimer College, 13350. (315) 866–4119
Ithaca
Ithaca Gay People's Center, 306 E. State St., 14850. (607) 277–0306
Cornell Gay Liberation, c/o Gay People's Center, 306 E. State St., 14850.
Jamestown
Lambda, Box 273, 14701. (716) 487–1876

Livingston Manor
Sullivan County Gay Liberation, c/o Tim, Box 191, 12758.
New York City
BRONX
Gay Integrated Group, Bronx Community College, 181 St. and University Ave., 10468.
Gay People at Lehman, Herbert Lehman College, Bedford Park Blvd., 10468.

BROOKLYN
Gay Hispanic Council of Boro Park, c/o Danny Beauchamp, 5619 Fourteenth Ave., 11219. (212) 494–9450
Gay Human Rights League of Kings County, Box 96, 2293 Bedford Ave., 11227. (212) 494–9450
Gay Liberation Front, Long Island University, c/o Student Activities, 365 Flatbush Ave., Extension, 12201.
Gay People at Brooklyn College, c/o Student Activities, LaGuardia Hall, Bedford Ave. and Ave. H., 11210. (212) 449–8432
Gay Students League of New York City Community College, Student Activities, 300 Jay St., 11201. (212) 824–6334
Gay Teachers Association, 204 Lincoln Place, 11217.
Mongoose Community Center Gay Group, 782 Union St., 11215. (212) 783–8819
Network Helpline, c/o Patricia Faber, 215 Willoughby Ave., Room 108, 11205.
Pratt Gay Union, Student Affairs, Pratt Institute, 11205. (212) 636–3505

MANHATTAN
Alcoholics Anonymous, 24 E. Twenty-second St., 10010. (212) 473–3067
Compass: Chelsea Coordinating Committee on Drug Addiction, Inc., 239 W. Nineteenth St., 10011. (212) 691–5710
Daughters of Bilitis at the Firehouse, 243 W. Twentieth St., 10011.
Eulenspiegel Society, Box 2783, Grand Central Station, 10017. (212) 254–2144
Faggot and Dyke Anarchists, 13 E. Seventeenth St., 6th Floor, 10003.
Faggot Effeminists, c/o Templar Press, Box 98 FDR Station, 10022.
Gay Activists Alliance, Box 2, Village Station, 10014. (212) 677–6090
Gay Men's Health Project, 74 Grove St., Room 2-RW, 10014.
Gay People at City College, Findlay Student Center, CCNY, Convent Ave. and W. 135th St., 10031. (212) 831–0851
Gay People at Columbia, 304 Earl Hall, 10027. (212) 280–3574, Ext. 29
Gay People at New School, 59 Christopher St., 10014.

Gay People's Union of New York University, Box 13, Loeb Student Center, 10012.

Gay Rights Action Coalition, 527 W. Forty-sixth St., Room 10, 10036. (212) 777–1381, 246–1479

Gay Speakers Bureau of Mattachine Society, 59 Christopher St., 10014. (212) 691–1068

Gay Workers Party, 339 Lafayette St., 10012.

Gay Youth, c/o Church of the Beloved Disciple, 384 W. Fourteenth St., 10014. (212) 691–1068

Hunter College Gay Men's Alliance, 695 Park Ave., Room 124, 10017. (212) 360–2123

Lambda Legal Defense and Education Fund, Inc., 145 E. Fifty-second St., 10022. (212) 758–1905

Lesbian Activists at Barnard College, Room 106, McIntosh Center, 10027.

Lesbian Feminist Liberation, Box 243, Village Station, 10014.

Liberation News Service, 160 Claremont Ave., 10027.

Long Island Gay Alliance, c/o Gay Activists Alliance, Box 2, Village Station, 10014. (516) 481–1929

Mattachine Society, 59 Christopher St., 10014. (212) 691–1066

National Coalition of Gay Activists, Box 3452 Grand Central Station, 10017. (212) 691–3625

National Gay Task Force, Suite 903, 80 Fifth Ave., 10011. (212) 741–1010

New York Alliance for the Eradication of VD, Inc., 93 Worth St., 10012.

New York Growth Center, 10 E. Twenty-ninth St., 10016.

New York State Coalition of Gay Organizations, c/o National Gay Task Force, 80 Fifth Ave., Suite 903, 10011.

Pan-Hellenic Council, 211 W. Twenty-second St., Apt. 2B, 10011. (212) 675–1728

Queen's Liberation Front, Box 538, 10009. (212) 489–1348

West Side Discussion Group, Box 611 Old Chelsea Station, 10011. (212) 675–0143

Woman's Action Alliance, Inc., 370 Lexington Ave., 10017.

QUEENS

Gay Community at Queens College, Student Activities, 11367.

Gay Human Rights League of Queens County, Box 1224, Flushing, 11352.

STATEN ISLAND

Gay Liberation of Staten Island Community College, Student Activities, 715 Ocean Terrace, 10301.

Gay Men's Collective, Richmond College, c/o Student Government, Room 542, 130 Stuyvesant Place, 10301. (212) 448–6835

Lesbians United, Richmond College, c/o Student Government, Room 542, 130 Stuyvesant Place, 10301. (212) 448–6835

Oneonta

People's Association for Gay Expression, Box 541, 13820.

Oswego

Gays for Human Liberation, Hewitt Union Bldg., Oswego State College, 13126.

Plattsburgh

Plattsburgh Gay Students Liberation, College Center, State University College, (518) 564–2165.

The Gays of Clinton County, T.G.O.C.C., Box G, 109 Margaret St., (518) 561–6863.

Potsdam

Potsdam-Canton Gay Community, College Union, State University College, 13676.

Poughkeepsie

Vassar Gay Liberation, Box 917, 12601.

Preston Hollow

Dyke, c/o Cowan, Box 90, 12469.

Purchase

Gay Awareness, c/o Emmett McGuire, SUNY at Purchase, 10577.

Rochester

Gay Alliance of the Genesee Valley, Inc., 713 Monroe Ave., 14607. (716) 244–8640

Gay Brotherhood of Rochester, 713 Monroe Ave., 14607 (716) 244–8640

Gay Liberation Front, University of Rochester, Box 6913, River Station, 14627. (716) 275–6181

Lesbian Resource Center, 713 Monroe Ave., 14607. (716) 244–9030

Rochester Gay Task Force, 2 Fuller Place, 14680. (716) 235–4961

Saratoga Springs

New York State Coalition of Gay Organizations, Box 690, 12866.

Skidmore Sapphic Society, c/o Casey Crabill, Skidmore College, 12866. (518) 584–5000

Stony Brook

Stony Brook Gay Student Union, SUNY Stony Brook, Stony Brook Union, 11794. (516) 246–7943

Syracuse

Gay Citizens Alliance of Syracuse, Box 57 Elmwood Station, 13207. (315) 476–2712

Lesbian Feminists of Syracuse, c/o 113 Concord Place, 13210. (315) 472–3735

Syracuse University Gay Student Services, 103 College Place, 2nd Floor, Suite 6, 13210. (315) 423–2081

White Plains

Gay Liberation of Westchester, Inc. (GLOW), Box 847, 10602. (914) WE7–1662

Westchester Gay Men's Association, c/o Wespac, 100 Mamaroneck Ave., 10601.

Woodstock

Woodstock Women's Center, 59A Tinker St., 12498.

NORTH CAROLINA —————————————————————

Chapel Hill

Female Liberation, Box 954, 27514.

Charlotte

Gay Liberation Front, c/o Brad Keistler, 1218 Myrtle Ave., 28203.

Durham

Carolina Gay Association, c/o Duke Gay Alliance, Box 7686 College Station, 27708.

Duke Gay Alliance, Box 7686 College Station, 27708. (919) 684–3043

Female Liberation, Box 954, 27514. (919) 929–1829

Lesbian Rap Group, c/o Duke Gay Alliance, Box 7686, College Station, 27708.

Triangle Area Lesbian Feminists, Box 2272, 27702.

Greenville

Eastern Gay Alliance, 1107 Evans St., 27834.

NORTH DAKOTA —————————————————————

Grand Forks

Aware, Box 1283, 58201.

OHIO ———————————————————————————

Akron

Akron University Gays, c/o Dr. Walter Sheppe, Dept. of Biology, University of Akron, 44325.

Athens

Gay Activist Alliance, c/o United Campus Ministry, 18 N. College St., 45701.

Bowling Green

Bowling Green Gay Union, Box 9, U. Hall, Bowling Green State University, 43402.

Cincinnati
Labyris, Box 6302, 45206.
University of Cincinnati Gay Society, c/o Student Affairs Office, 240 Tangeman University Center, 45221. (513) 475–6876
Cleveland
Dykes You Know Everywhere, 1688 Glenmont Rd., Cleveland Heights, 04418. (216) 371–1697
Gay Education & Research, Box 6177, 44101.
Columbus
Columbus Gay Activists Alliance, 323 Ohio Union, 1739 N. High St., 43210. (614) 422–9212
Gay Women Sapphonified, c/o Women's Liberation, 1739 N. High St., 43210. (614) 866–5274
Society for Individual Rights of Ohio, Inc., Box 9761, 43206.
Dayton
Sappho's Army, c/o Dayton Women's Center, 1309 N. Main St., 45406. (513) 228–1203
Kent
Kent Gay Liberation Front, 233 Student Center, Kent State University, 44242. (216) 692–2068
Rockbridge
Society for Individual Rights of Ohio, Inc., Rt. 1, Box 298, 43149.
Toledo
Now Sexuality/Lesbian Task Force, 1049 Curtis St., 43609.
Pro/Toledo: Personal Rights Organization, Box 4642, Old West End Station, 43620. (419) 243–9351
Yellow Springs
Antioch Gay Liberation, Antioch College Student Union, 45387. (513) 767–7331, Ext. 217
Youngstown
Mattachine Society, Box 2522, 45507.
Personal Rights Organization, Box 2522, 45507.

OKLAHOMA ——————————————————————————————
Ada
Daughters of Bilitis, Box 162, 74820.
Oklahoma City
Libertarians for Gay Rights, 1206 N.W. Fortieth St., 73118.

OREGON ———————————————————————————————
Eugene
Gay People's Alliance, University of Oregon, EMU Suite I, 97401. (503) 686–3327

Lesbian Rap Group, c/o Women's Center, Second and Washington Sts., 97401.

One Step Beyond, 323 E. Twelfth St., 97401.

Klamath Falls

Klamath Gay Union, The Church, 428 S. Ninth St., 97601.

Oregon Gay Political Caucus, 428 S. Ninth St., 97601.

Portland

Gay Community Center/Second Foundation, Box 4183, 97208.

Gay Liberation Front, Portland State College, c/o Steve Fulmer, #403, 1232 S.W. Jefferson, 97201.

Gay People's Alliance, Room 422, Smith Center, Portland State University, 97207. (503) 229–4474

Gay Public Employees Federation, 1329 S.W. Fourteenth St., Apt. 30-8, 97201. (503) 223–8362

Gay Student Affairs Board, Room 438, Smith Center, Portland State University, 97201. (503) 229–4458

Gay Teens, c/o Moon Brothers Collective, 729 S.E. Thirty-third Ave., 97214. (503) 238–0146

Gay Women's Liberation, Portland State University, c/o Women's Studies, 97207.

Lambda House, 1867 S.W. Fourteenth Ave., 97201.

Oregon Gay Political Caucus, 118 W. Burnside, 97214. (503) 227–6550

Portland Association for Gay Equality, 118 W. Burnside, 97209. (503) 227–0432

Portland Gay Liberation Front Communications Committee, 4226 N. Montana Ave., 97217. (503) 287–7894

Portland Town Council, 320 S.W. Stark St., Room 303, 97204. (503) 227–2765

Second Foundation of Oregon, c/o 7705 S.W. Alden, 97223. (503) 246–3021

Salem

Oregon Gay Political Caucus, 1065 E. Twenty-second St., N.E., 97310.

Salem Group, c/o Portland Town Council, 320 S.W. Stark St., Room 303, Portland, 97204.

Troutdale

United Order: The Key, Box 412, 97060. (503) 659–9254

PENNSYLVANIA————————————————————————————

Bethlehem

Lehigh Valley Homophile Organization (LE-HI-HO), Box 1003, Moravian Station, 18018.

Harrisburg
Gay Community Services, Box 297, Federal Square Station, 17108. (717) 232–2027
Indiana
Homophiles of Indiana University of Pennsylvania, Box 1588, Indiana University, 15701.
Lancaster
Gays United Lancaster, 3002 Marietta Ave., 17601. (717) 898–2876
Philadelphia
Caucus of Gay Public Health Workers, c/o Dr. Lear, 206 N. Thirty-fifth St., 19104.
Gay Activist Alliance, Box 15786, 19103. (215) 456–0217
Gay Civil Servants, D. Rolla c/o PA Social Services Union, 210 S. Thirteenth St., 19107.
Gay Community Center Committee of Philadelphia, Inc., Box 15748, 19103. (215) 978–5700
Gay Students at Temple, Room 205, Student Activities Center, Thirteenth and Montgomery Sts., 12122. (215) 787–7902
Gay Youth National Committee, Box 15786, Middle City Station, 19103. (215) 787–7902, 555–2646
Gays at Penn, c/o Christian Association, 3601 Locust Walk, 19104. (215) 386–1610
Radical Queens, c/o Box 15786, 19103.
S.M. Society of Philadelphia, Box 15786, 19103. (215) 723–8276, 545–2646
Task Force on Gay Liberation, American Library Association, Box 2383, 19103. (215) 382–3222
Women's Committee, Gay Activists Alliance, Box 15786, 19103.
Pittsburgh
Gay Alternatives, Box 10236, 15232. (412) 363–0594
Gay Students at Pitt, Box 819 Schenley, University of Pittsburgh, 15260. (412) 624–5944
Lesbian Feminists, c/o Persad Center, 5100 Centre Ave., 15232.
Reading
Gay Coordinating Society, Reading, Box 5, Fleetwood, 19522.
Shippensburg
Shippensburg Students for Gay Rights, c/o CUB, Shippensburg State College, 17257.
State College
Homophiles of Penn State, Box 218, State College, 16801. (814) 863–0296

Swarthmore
Swarthmore Gay Liberation, Swarthmore College, 19081. (215) 978–2500

RHODE ISLAND
Kingston
Kingston Gay Liberation, Memorial Union, University of Rhode Island, 02881. (401) 792–5817
Pawtucket
Framingham Unicorn Society, c/o Box 413, 02862.
Providence
Brown Gay Students Organization, Box 49, Student Activities Office, Brown University, 02912.
Rhode Island College Gay Alliance, c/o Rhode Island College Student Union, Mt. Pleasant Ave., 02907. (401) 831–6600, Ext. 474

TENNESSEE
Knoxville
Gay Liberation Front, University of Tennessee, Room 307-B, U.T. Center, 37916.
Knoxville Lesbian Collective, 2911 Jersey Ave., 37919. (617) 532–7288
Knoxville Men's Resource Center, Box 8060, U.T. Station, 37916.
Memphis
Gay Men's Discussion Group, c/o Northeast Mental Health Center, 3618 Summer Ave., 38122.

TEXAS
Austin
Austin Gay Liberation, Box 8107, University Station, 78712. (512) 476–2820, 472–0810
Austin Lesbian Organization, The Alley, 710 W. Twenty-fourth St., 78705. (512) 472–3053
Gay People of Austin, 2330 Guadalupe St., 78705. (512) 477–6699
Gay Political Committee, Box 1255, 78767.
Womanspace, 2330 Guadalupe St., 78705. (512) 846–5903, 476–8058
Corpus Christi
Gay Organization, Box 675, 78403. (512) 991–0940
Dallas
Dallas Daughters of Bilitis, Box 1242, 75221. (214) 742–1947
Gay Community Service Center, 3834 Ross Ave., 75204. (214) 826–2192

Fort Worth
AURA (Awareness, Unity & Research Association), Box 7318, 76111.
(817) 838–2095
Daughters of Bilitis, Box 1564, 76101. (817) 924–8598
Texas Gay Task Force, Northern Region, c/o AURA, Box 7318, 76111.
Houston
Gay Activists Alliance of Houston, Box 441, University Center, University of Houston, 77004. (713) 749–4100
Gay Liberation, University of Houston, Box 65, University Center, 77004. (713) 749–4124, 529–6258
Gay Political Committee, Box 16041, 77022.
Houston N.O.W. Sexuality & Lesbian Task Force, c/o Women's Center, 3602 Milam, 77002. (713) 524–5743
Texas Gay Task Force, c/o Integrity, Box 16041, 77022.
United Homophile Organization, c/o Integrity, Box 16041, 77022.
Lubbock
Lubbock Gay Awareness, Box 4002, 79409. (806) 762–4974

UTAH ————————————————————————————————
Salt Lake City
Gay Community Center, 11 S. 400, West, 84101.

VERMONT ————————————————————————————————
Burlington
Gay in Vermont, Box 3216, North Burlington Station, 05401. (802)
862–2397
Gay Student Union, Billings Center, University of Vermont, 05401.
(802) 656–4173
Plainfield
Gay Students Organization, Box 501, Goddard College, 05667.

VIRGINIA ————————————————————————————————
Charlottesville
Gay Student Union, Peabody Hall, University of Virginia, 22901.
Richmond
Gay Awareness in Perspective, Box 12465, 23241.
Gay Liberation Front, c/o Kenny Pederson, 505 Brookside Blvd., 23327.
(703) 266–2691
Williamsburg
Gay Liberation Group, College of William and Mary, Campus Center,
23185.

WASHINGTON ——————————————————————————————
Bellingham
Gay People's Alliance, Viking Union, Room 212, Western Washington
    State University, 98225. (206) 676–3460
Mountain Terrace
Gay Parents' Legal Research Group, Box 82, 98043.
Pullman
Gay Awareness, Washington State University, Compton Union, 3rd
    floor, 99163.
Seattle
Feminist Coordinating Council, 5649 Eleventh St., N.E., 98105. (206)
    525–5829, 325–8258
Gay Community Center, 1726 Sixteenth Ave., 98122. (206) 322–2000
Gay Community Social Service, Box 22228, 98122. (206) 324–3571
Gay Feminists Coalition, c/o Metropolitan Community Church, Box
    12020, 98112. (206) 324–3571
Gay Liberation Front, c/o Seattle Gay Alliance, Box 1170, 98111.
Gay Students Association, Box 96, HUB (FK-10), University of Washing-
    ton, 98195. (206) 543–6106
Lesbian Mothers National Defense Fund, 2446 Lorentz Place North,
    98109. (206) 324–3571, 282–5798
Lesbian Resource Center, 4224 University Ave. N.E., 98105. (206) 632–
    4747
Seattle Gay Alliance, Box 1170, 98111. (206) 323–6969
The Woman's Woman, 910 E. Pike St., 98122.

WISCONSIN ——————————————————————————————
Madison
Gay Activists Alliance, c/o Renaissance of Madison, Box 687, 53701.
Madison Gay Center, 1001 University Ave., 53715. (608) 257–7575
Renaissance of Madison, Box 687, 53701. (608) 257–7575
Menasha
Fox Valley Gay Alliance, Box 332, 54952. (414) 233–2948
Milwaukee
Gay Alcoholics Anonymous, Newman Center, 2528 E. Linnwood,
    53211. (414) 271–5273
Gay People's Union, Box 92203, 53202. (414) 271–5273
Grapevine, c/o Women's Center, 2211 E. Kenwood Blvd., 53211.
Milwaukee Gay Community Services Center, 2211 E. Kenwood Blvd.,
    53211. (414) 263–4110
Milwaukee Teens, c/o GPU, Box 92203, 53202. (414) 271–5273
University Wisconsin-Milwaukee Gay Student Association, Box 10,
    Student Union, 53211.

APPENDIX C

Gay Church Groups

Some communities that do not have independent gay organizations — and others that do — have church-affiliated groups that offer health referrals, and other services, including religious counseling, to homosexually active people. Many maintain lists of sympathetic local psychologists, psychiatrists, and other counselors.

ALASKA
Anchorage
Metropolitan Community Church/Anchorage, Box 3-091, 99501. (907) 272–1715, 277–0340

ARIZONA
Coolidge
Gay Episcopalian Caucus, Box 1631, 85228.
Phoenix
Metropolitan Community Church, Box 21064, 85036. (602) 271–0125
Tucson
Metropolitan Community Church, Box 50412, 85703. (602) 622–0330

CALIFORNIA
Berkeley
Gay Seminarians, 2441 Leconte, 94709.
Psychedelic Venus Church, Box 4163 Sather Gate Station, 94704.
St. Procopius Orthodox Catholic Church, Box 40482, 94140. (415) 848–0800
Costa Mesa
Christ Chapel: Metropolitan Community Church in Orange County, 215 E. Twenty-third St., 92627. (714) 548–5046, 833–3274, 642–4253
Escondido
Metropolitan Community Church Palomar, Box 228, 92025. (714) 746–5660

Fresno

Fellowship of the New Covenant, 2542 E. Belmont, 93727. (209) 268–2011

Fresno Garden Metropolitan Community Church, Box 772, 93710. (415) 225–8806

Long Beach

Dignity, Box 7305, 90807.

Metropolitan Community Church, 785 Junipero Ave., 90804.

Los Angeles

Beth Chaymin Chadashim, 1050 S. Hill St., 90015. (213) 748–5313

Dignity, Box 6161, 90055. (213) 469–3898

Integrity/Los Angeles, 4767 Hillsdale Drive, 90032. (213) 225–7471

Lutherans Concerned for Gay People, Box 19114A, 90019. (213) 663–7816

Metropolitan Community Church, 1050 South Hill St., 90015. (213) 748–0121

The People's Church, 1961 N. Argyle Ave., #18, 92805. (714) 533–2536

Universal Fellowship of Metropolitan Community Churches, 1050 S. Hill St., 90015. (213) 221–0342

Monterey

Metropolitan Community Church/Monterey, 1154 Second St. 93940. (408) 375–2338

North Hollywood

Metropolitan Community Church in the Valley, 11717 Victory Blvd., 91606. (213) 762–1133

Oakland

East Bay Metropolitan Community Church, 2624 West St., 94612. (415) 763–1592

Oceanside

Palomar Metropolitan Community Church, Box 237, 92089. (714) 746–5660

Pomona

Metropolitan Community Church Pomona, 243 Acacia St., 91767.

Riverside

Dignity of the Inland Empire, Box 20081, 92506.

Trinity Metropolitan Community Church, Box 2451, 92506. (714) 682–7445

Sacramento

Dignity/Sacramento, Inc., Box 9643, 95823. (916) 422–6305

Metropolitan Community Church Sacramento, 2741 Thirty-fourth St., 95817.

San Diego
Dignity, Box 19071, 92119. (714) 448–8384
Integrity, Rev. Dr. H. C. Lazenby, 4645 W. Talmadge Dr., 92116.
Metropolitan Community Church, Box 33291, 92103. (714) 239–3723
San Francisco
Achavah: Jewish Gay Union, Box 5528, 94101. (415) 451–8743, 666–6227
Church of Androgynous, Box 6437, 94101.
Committee of Concern, c/o Friends Meetinghouse, 2160 Lake St., 94121. (415) 431–3344
Council on Religion and the Homosexual, 83 Sixth St., 94103. (415) 781–1570
Dignity/Bay Area, Box 5127, 94101.
Integrity, c/o Jim Frooks, 1256 Page St., #1, 94117.
Metropolitan Community Church, 1076 Guerrero, 94102. (415) 285–0392
Ministry of Concern, Box 386, 94101. (415) 864–8205
St. Timothy's Chapel, 474 Eddy St., 94102. (415) 885–4534
The People's Church, 135 Albion St., 94110. (415) 863–3203
San Jose
Integrity, Box 6444, 95150
Metropolitan Community Church of San Jose, Box 24126, 95154. (408) 267–3211
Santa Monica
West Bay Metropolitan Community Church, 1260 Eighteenth St., 90403.
Stockton
Metropolitan Community Church, 2606 N. Wilson Way, 95205.
Venice
The Feminista WICCA, 422 Lincoln Blvd., 90291. (213) 399–3919
Ventura
Metropolitan Community Church, 362 N. Ventura Ave., 93001.

COLORADO ————————————————————————————
Boulder
Dignity Boulder, Box 1402, 80302.
Denver
Integrity, Rev. Thomas Dobbs, 1958 Emerson St., 80218.
Metropolitan Community Church of the Rockies, Box 9536, 80209. (303) 831–4787

CONNECTICUT————————————————————————————
Hartford
Church of the Eternal Flame Universal, 320 Farmington Ave., 06105.
(203) 527–5612
Metropolitan Community Church/Hartford, Box 514, 06101. (203) 522–8651

DISTRICT OF COLUMBIA ————————————————————————
Dignity/Washington, 1616 Forty-fourth St., N.W., 20007.
Integrity/Washington, D.C., Dr. Robert Bissell, 11917 PH-1 Winterthur
Lane, Reston, Va., 22091.
Jewish Gays of Baltimore/Washington Area, Box 34038, 20034. (202)
547–4562
Metropolitan Community Church of Washington, D.C., 945 G St., N.W.,
20001. (202) 232–6333
Unitarian Gay Community All Souls Unitarian Church, 16 Harvard,
N.W., 20009. (202) 722–0439
Universal Fellowship of Metropolitan Community Churches Washing-
ton Office, 110 Maryland Ave., N.E., Suite 210, 20002. (202) 543–2260

FLORIDA ————————————————————————————————
Clearwater
Dignity/Sun Coast, Box 2811, 33516.
Fort Lauderdale
All Saints Reformed Orthodox Church, 808 W. Sunrise Blvd. (305)
763–5774
Dignity/Gold Coast, Box 8503, 33310.
Metropolitan Community Church, Box 1457, 33302. (305) 462–2004
Universal New Age Church, 1331 N.E. Fourth Ave., 33311.
Fort Myers
Metropolitan Community Church, Box 6252, 33902. (813) 995–5884
Jacksonville
Dignity/Jacksonville, Box 5012, 32207.
Integrity, Dr. Robert Ragland, Box 5524, 32207.
Metropolitan Community Church, Box 291, 32201. (904) 354–1318
Largo
King of Peace Metropolitan Community Church, 1050 Parkview Lane,
33540. (813) 581–5587
Miami
Metropolitan Community Synagogue of Greater Miami, Box 330132,
33133. (305) 758–7190

Metropolitan Community Church, Box 370963, 33137. (305) 758–7190
Orlando
Metropolitan Community Church of Orlando, Box 6872, 32803.
Tampa
Metropolitan Community Church, 2904 Concordia Ave., 33609. (813)
839–5939

GEORGIA ————————————————————————————
Atlanta
Dignity, Box 77013, 30309.
Integrity/Atlanta, Dr. Ara Destourian, Department of History, West
Georgia College, Carrollton, 30117.
Metropolitan Community Church, 800 N. Highland Ave., N.E., 30306.
(404) 872–2246
Hampton
Living Word Chapel, Box 468, 30228. (404) 872–2013

HAWAII ————————————————————————————
Honolulu
Metropolitan Community Church — Center, Box 15825, 96815. (808)
922–3029

ILLINOIS ————————————————————————————
Chicago
Chicago Gay Seminarians and Clergy, Box 2073, 60690. (312) 528–3064
Dignity, Box 11262, 60611. (312) 281–8094
Ecumenical Religious Committee, c/o Mary Houlihan, 1221 W. Sherwin,
60626. (312) 262–9609
Gay Jewish Group, c/o Tvsi Goodman, 3337 N. Halsted St., 60657. (312)
549–0901
Integrity/Chicago, Inc., Box 2516, 60302. (312) 386–1470
Lutherans Concerned for Gay People, c/o Kris Warmouth, 1545 E. Six-
tieth St., Apt. 415, 60637.
Metropolitan Community Church: Good Shepherd Parish, Box 2392,
60690. (312) 922–5822
Presbyterian Gay Caucus, Box 2073, 60690. (312) 528–3064
Unitarian Universalist Gay Caucus, c/o First Unitarian Church, 5650 S.
Woodland Ave., 60637. (312) 324–4100
Unity Clergy/Gay Rap, c/o Mary Houlihan, 1221 W. Sherwin, 60626.
(312) 262–9609
La Grange
Holy Covenant Community Church, Box 9134, 60690. (312) 274–5582

Quincy
Metropolitan Community Church/Illiamo, 16 Skyview Ct., Keokuk, 62301. (312) 425–2632

INDIANA ———————————————————————————————
Fort Wayne
Metropolitan Community Church, Box 5443, 46805. (812) 432–5941
Indianapolis
Dignity, Box 831, 46206.
Metropolitan Community Church, 1940 N. Delaware, 46202. (317) 925–0413
South Bend
Metropolitan Community Church, Box 201, 46205. (317) 925–0851
Michiana Metropolitan Community Church, 1527 Kemble Ave., 46613. (219) 287–2552

IOWA ————————————————————————————————————
Des Moines
Metropolitan Community Church, Box 4546, 50306.

KANSAS ———————————————————————————————————
Kansas City
Dignity, Box 1242, 66117.
Wichita
Metropolitan Community Church, Box 2639, 67201. (316) 681–1573

KENTUCKY ————————————————————————————————
Lexington
Integrity, Box 383 University Station, 40506. (606) 272–2854
Metropolitan Community Church — Lexington, 507 N. Broadway, 40507. (606) 233–1082
Louisville
Dignity of Louisville, Box 4123, 40204.

LOUISIANA ————————————————————————————————
Baton Rouge
Dignity, Box 2465, 70821.
New Orleans
Dignity of New Orleans, Box 7133, Metairie, 70011.
Metropolitan Community Church, 1934 Burgundy, 70117. (504) 945–5976

MARYLAND
Baltimore
Dignity, 761 Hamburg St., 21230. (301) 727–0915
Metropolitan Community Church of Baltimore, Box 1145, 21203. (301) 366–1415

MASSACHUSETTS
Boston
B'nai Haskalah, 131 Cambridge St., 02114. (617) 265–6409
Dignity/Boston, 1105 Boylston St., 02215.
Integrity/Boston, Box 2582, 02208. (617) 846–6580
Metropolitan Community Church, 131 Cambridge St., 02114. (617) 523–7664
Rev. Paul R. Shanley, 128 Tremont St., Braintree, 02184. (617) 043–5731
Unitarian Universalist Gay Caucus, Box 1000, Gay Community News, 22 Bromfield St., 02108. (617) 282–4977
Unitarian-Universalist Office for Gay Concerns, 25 Beacon St., 02108. (617) 742–2100
Cambridge
Church of the Stranger, Box 291, MIT Branch, 02139.
Lowell
Dignity/Merrimack Valley, Box 348, 01853. (617) 851–6711
Springfield
Dignity, Box 488, Forest Park Station, 01108.
Worcester
Metropolitan Community Church, 64 Chandler St., 01601. (617) 756–0730

MICHIGAN
Detroit
Dignity, 2846 Seventeenth St., 48216. (313) 894–1064
Metropolitan Community Church, Box 34874, 48234. (313) 869–8159
Southfield
Metropolitan Community Church, Box 1017, 48705. (313) 869–8159
Wyandotte
Old Catholic Archdiocese, 3802 Tenth St., 48192. (313) 284–6624

MINNESOTA
Minneapolis
Committee of Concern, 3208 Portland Ave., S., 55407.
Dignity/Twin Cities, Box 3565, 55403. (612) 341–3392
Integrity, Frank R. Eggers, 26 Arthur Ave., Box 203, 55414.

Lutherans Concerned for Gay People, Box 3590, Upper Nicollet Station, 55403. (612) 871–1190

Metropolitan Community Church of the Twin Cities, Box 8402, 55408. (612) 338–2773

Minnesota Council for the Church and the Homophile, 122 W. Franklin, Room 508, 55404. (612) 335–1281

MISSOURI ——————————————————————————

Joplin

Metropolitan Community Church, 207 W. Fourth St., Suite #321–323. (471) 781–9494

Kansas City

Metropolitan Community Church of Greater Kansas City, Box 5206, 64112. (816) 921–5754

St. Louis

Dignity/St. Louis, Box 23093, 63159

Metropolitan Community Church of Greater St. Louis, Box 3147, 63131. (314) 361–7284

NEBRASKA ——————————————————————————

Lincoln

Lincoln-Omaha Council on Religion and the Homosexual, Box 2323, Station B, 68502.

Omaha

First Metropolitan Community Church of Nebraska, 803 N. Twentieth St., 68102. (402) 345–2563

NEVADA ———————————————————————————

Las Vegas

American Eastern Orthodox Church — St. George Monastery, 1580 Bledsoe Lane, 89110.

Metropolitan Community Church, Box 4798, 89106.

NEW JERSEY —————————————————————————

Irvington

Dignity/Metropolitan New Jersey, Box 337, 07111.

Jersey City

United Interfaith Church, 132 Bergen, 07305. (201) 659–3840

Kearney

Church of the New Revelation, Box 510, 07032.

NEW MEXICO———————————————————————————
Albuquerque
Metropolitan Community Church, Box 26554, 87125. (505) 299–0512

NEW YORK ————————————————————————————
Albany
United Methodist Gay Caucus, c/o Ernest Reaugh, 17A Old Hickory Rd.,
12204.
Buffalo
Stonewall Community Church, 25 Calumet Place, 14222.
Latham
Unitarian Universalist Gay Caucus, 10 Eberle Rd., 12110.
New York City
BROOKLYN
 Committee of Concern, c/o Steve Kirkman, 357 Dean St., 11217.
 Metropolitan Community Church of Brooklyn, 50 Monroe Place,
 11201.
MANHATTAN
 Beth Chayim Chadashim, 372 Central Park West, Apt. 19U, 10025.
 (212) 850–8022
 Celtic Order of the Silver Unicorn, 211 W. Twenty-second St., 2-B,
 10011. (212) 675–1728
 Church of the Beloved Disciple, 348 W. Fourteenth St., 10014. (212)
 242–6616
 Congregation of Beth Simchat Torah, Box 1270, GPO, 10001. (212)
 749–8659
 Committee of Friends on Bisexuality, 703 Hastings Hall, 600 W.
 122nd St., 10027. (212) 866–8986
 Dignity/New York, Box 1554 FDR Station, 10022.
 Episcopalian Gay Caucus, c/o National Gay Task Force, 80 Fifth Ave.,
 Room 903, 10011.
 Integrity/New York, 31 Stuyvesant St., 10003. (212) 982–3559
 Metropolitan Community Church, Box 1517, 10001. (212) 691–7428
 Metropolitan Community Church Hispaña, Box 110, 10009. (212)
 777–6838, 781–2177
 The People's Church Community of the Love of Christ, 339 Lafayette
 St., 10012. (212) 431–6440, 228–0322
 United Church of Christ Gay Caucus in New York, c/o Milton
 Lounsberry, Apt. 2-D, 421 E. Seventy-eighth St., 10021. (212) 628–
 2038
Rochester
Dignity/Rochester, Box 8295, 14617. (716) 458–8628

Rochester Community Church, 65 Edmonds St., 14607.
Syracuse
Gay Community Ministries, Box 57 Elmwood Station, 13207. (315)
478–5225

OHIO————————————————————————————————————
Akron
Dignity/Akron, Box 3501, 44301.
Metropolitan Community Church, Box 563, 44309.
Cincinnati
Dignity/Cincinnati, Box 98, Bellevue, Ky. 41073.
Integrity/SW Ohio and Northern Kentucky, Box 24096, 45224.
Metropolitan Community Church, Box 39235, 45239. (513) 591–0303
Cleveland
Community of Celebration, Box 18226, 44118.
Dignity/Cleveland, Box 18479, 44118. (216) 791–0942
Fellowship Metropolitan Community Church, Box 99234, 44199.
Lutherans Concerned for Gay People, Box 22, Hamma School of Theology, 45504.
Dayton
Dignity/Dayton, Box 1283, 54501.
Toledo
Metropolitan Community Church, Box 5583, 43613. (419) 255–1714
Youngstown
Dignity/Youngstown, Box 4202, Austintown, 44515.

OKLAHOMA————————————————————————————————
Oklahoma City
Christ the King Metropolitan Community Church, 401 S.E. Twenty-second St., 73129. (405) 632–3625
Tulsa
Metropolitan Community Church, Box 4187, 74104. (918) 939–0417

OREGON ————————————————————————————————
Canby
United Order, 27700 S. Oglesby Rd., 97013. (503) 266–5660
Portland
Eastwood Community Church, 4620 E. Sixty-seventh Ave., 97206. (503)
238–0018, 232–4925
Springfield
Metropolitan Community Church of the Willamette Valley, 160 N.
Twentieth St., #8. (503) 746–7427

PENNSYLVANIA————————————————————————————
Erie
Dignity, 331 W. Fourth St., 16507.
Harrisburg
Dignity/Central Pennsylvania, Box 297 Federal Square Station, 17108.
Philadelphia
Beth Zion Israel, Box 15786, 19103.
Dignity/Philadelphia, 250 S. Twelfth St., 19107.
Gay Pagans & Atheists, Box 15083, 19147.
Hosanna Christian Community, c/o Christian Association, 3601 Locust Walk, C-8, 19104.
Integrity/Philadelphia, c/o Rev. John Lenhardt, St. Mary's Episcopal Church, 3601 Locust Walk, Hamilton Village, 19104. (215) 726–1089
Metropolitan Community Church of Philadelphia, Box 8174, 19101. (215) 877–3384
Society of Friends Committee on Homosexuality, 1520 Race St., 19102.
United Church of Christ Gay Caucus, Box 6315, 19131.
Pittsburgh
Dignity/Pittsburgh, Box 991, 15230.
First Unitarian Church, Ellsworth & Moorehead Ave., 15213. (415) 621–8008
Metropolitan Community Church, Box 9045, 15224. (412) 683–2459
University Park
Metropolitan Community Church, 1798 N. Atherton St., #11, 16801. (814) 234–8649

RHODE ISLAND ——————————————————————————————
Providence
Dignity/Providence, Box 2231, Pawtucket, 02861. (401) 724–0171
Metropolitan Community Church, 63 Chapin Ave., 02903. (401) 274–1693

SOUTH CAROLINA—————————————————————————————
Columbia
Metropolitan Community Church, Box 11181, 29211.

TENNESSEE——————————————————————————————————
Nashville
Metropolitan Community Church of Christ the King, Box 187, 37202. (615) 255–0893

TEXAS————————————————————————————————
Austin
Integrity/Austin, Box 14056, 78761.
Dallas
Dignity/Dallas–Fort Worth, Box 813, Arlington, 76010.
Metropolitan Community Church, 3834 Ross Ave., 75204. (214) 826–0291
Fort Worth
Agape Metropolitan Community Church, 251 Vacek, 76107. (817) 332–5008
Grand Prairie
Metropolitan Community Church, Box 718, 75050. (214) 436–6865
Houston
Dignity/Houston, Box 66821, 77006.
Integrity/Houston, Box 16041, 77002. (713) 523–4609
Lutherans Concerned for Gay People, Box 70282, 77007.
Metropolitan Community Church, Box 13731, 77019. (713) 526–9434

UTAH ————————————————————————————————
Salt Lake City
Grace Christian Church, c/o Ron Linde, 2510 Glenmare St., 84106.
Lutherans Concerned for Gay People, Box 15592, 84115.
Metropolitan Community Church, Box 11607, 84111. (801) 531–9434

WASHINGTON ————————————————————————————
Seattle
Dignity/Seattle, 1726 Sixteenth Ave., 98102.
Metropolitan Community Church of Seattle, Box 12020, 98112. (206) 325–1872

WISCONSIN ————————————————————————————
Milwaukee
Council for Religion and the Homosexual, c/o GPU, Box 92203, 53202.
Dignity/Milwaukee, Box 597, 53201. (414) 276–5218
St. Nicholas Orthodox Parish, 1155 N. Twenty-first St., 53233. (414) 342–1722

APPENDIX D

Telephone Information and
Referral Services

Many organizations maintain telephone services that provide information on sexual matters and referrals to clinics, physicians, and counselors. Some of these services aim specifically at homosexually active people, others at the general population; the former often provide information and referrals in a variety of nonsexual areas — for example, civil rights litigation relating to discrimination based on sexual activity and/or orientation.

The most far-reaching of these telephone services is Operation Venus, the toll-free nationwide venereal disease consultation and referral service. It is a program of the United States Alliance for Eradication of Venereal Disease, established by a consortium of thirty well-known professional, civic, and special-interest groups including the American Academy of Family Physicians, the National Congress of Parents and Teachers, the American Red Cross, the American Junior Chamber of Commerce, and the American Legion. It is funded mainly by the venereal disease division of the Center for Disease Control, U.S. Public Health Service.

Operation Venus operates its phones twenty-four hours a day, offering information about sexually transmitted diseases and referring callers to nearby clinics, outpatient departments of general hospitals, or private practitioners. In addition, the organization regularly advises the physicians and institutions on its list about the latest findings and recommendations of the Center for Disease Control. When a physician or institution encounters a diagnostic or treatment problem that cannot be solved, Venus recruits expert consultants, who advise without charge.

The Operation Venus phone numbers:
   Toll-free nationwide, except in Pennsylvania: 800–523–1885
   Toll-free in Pennsylvania: 800–462–4966
   In Area Code 215 (Philadelphia and vicinity): 564–6969

CALIFORNIA ─────────────────────────────

Berkeley
Berkeley Gay Switchboard (415) 848–0800, 848–9583
Fresno
Gay Hotline (209) 224–8806
Los Angeles
Hotline (213) 464–7485
Women's Switchboard (213) 388–3491
San Francisco
Help Line (415) 771–3366
Men's Switchboard (415) 922–5247
Women's Switchboard (415) 431–1414

DISTRICT OF COLUMBIA ───────────────────

Gay Information and Assistance (202) 363–3881, 544–8042
Gay Switchboard of Washington, D.C. (202) 387–3777
Lesbian Switchboard (608) 257–7575
Switchboard (202) 387–6895

GEORGIA ─────────────────────────────────
Atlanta
Gay Help Line (404) 874–4400

ILLINOIS ────────────────────────────────
Chicago
Chicago Women's Liberation Union (312) 953–6808
Gay Switchboard & Information Exchange (312) 929–9180

KANSAS ──────────────────────────────────
Wichita
People's Help Line (316) 686–2155

MASSACHUSETTS ──────────────────────────
Amherst
Hotline (413) 545–0154
Boston
Gay Hotline (617) 426–4469
Cambridge
Hotline (617) 876–7528
Haverhill
Northern Essex Community College Gay Line (617) 327–0929

Salem
Gay Hotline (617) 754–0594

MICHIGAN————————————————————————
Ann Arbor
Gay Hotline (313) 761–2044
Detroit
Gay Switchboard (313) 577–3450

NEBRASKA ————————————————————————
Lincoln
Gay Rap Line (402) 475–5710

NEW JERSEY ————————————————————————
Princeton
Gay Switchboard and Information Service (609) 921–2565

NEW YORK ————————————————————————
Hempstead
Middle Earth Switchboard (516) 292–0100
Manhattan
Gay Switchboard (212) 924–4036
Lesbian Switchboard (212) 741–2610
Syracuse
Gay Switchboard (315) 476–2712

OHIO————————————————————————————
Cincinnati
Switchboard (513) 475–6876

PENNSYLVANIA————————————————————————
Harrisburg
Gay Switchboard (717) 234–0328
Philadelphia
Gay Switchboard (215) 978–5700
Lesbian Hotline (215) 725–2001
Women's Switchboard (215) 563–8599
Pittsburgh
Gay Information (412) 363–0594

TEXAS————————————————————————————
Austin
Womanspace Switchboard (512) 846–5903, 476–8058

Dallas
Gayline of Dallas (214) 241–4118
Fort Worth
Switchboard (817) 338–0128
Houston
Crisis Hotline (713) 228–1505
San Antonio
Gay Switchboard (512) 733–7300

VERMONT ————————————————————————
Vermont Gay Women (802) 862–7770
Women's Switchboard (802) 862–5504, 863–3237

WASHINGTON ————————————————————————
Seattle
Assault Hotline (206) 329–HELP
Crisis Line (206) 329–8707
Radical Women (206) 329–8707
Women's Switchboard (206) 329–6500

WISCONSIN ————————————————————————
Madison
Gay Switchboard and Information Service (608) 257–7575
Lesbian Switchboard (608) 257–7378

Index

Abscess, 81, 117
Acupuncture, as impotence treatment, 146–147
Addison's disease, 137
Adrenal glands, 137
Adrenogenital syndrome, 166
Age, as V.D. factor, 8
Alcoholic beverages, 41, 69, 77, 138
Aldomet, 137
Alimentary canal, 72
Allergic reactions, 39, 40, 53, 63, 150; to metronidazole, 49; to N.S.U., 39, 40; to nystatin, 53
Amebiasis, 80–83, 84; diagnosis of, 82; proctitis and, 116; statistics on, 81; symptoms of, 82; treatment of, 83
Amebic dysentery. See Amebiasis
Ampicillin, 34
Amylnitrate, 144–145
Anal fissure, 113
Analgesics, 117
Analingus, 70, 71, 78, 83
Anemia, 137
Anesthesia, 40, 96
Animals: homosexuality among, 143–144; V.D. transmitted by, 104
Anorectal gonorrhea, 33
Anorectal passage: amebiasis and, 80; damage to, 148; fecal contamination and, 84; hygiene and, 119–120; N.S.V. and, 44, 46; sexual injury to, 108–120; trichomoniasis and, 50;

viral hepatitis and, 78
Antibiotics, 14, 116; moniliasis and, 53, 54; for rectal abscesses, 117; to prevent V.D., 50; prostatitis and, 85; V.D. and, 6
Antihistamine, 92
Anus, 12, 13, 151; abscesses of, 117; chancroid and, 66; foreign objects in, 114–115; gonorrhea and, 30, 32, 35; hepatitis and, 99; syphilis and, 23; warts and, 93, 94, 95
Appetite loss, 16; with gonorrhea, 33; with syphilis, 9; with viral hepatitis, 76
Astruc, John, 10
Aurelian, Laure, 101
"Australia Antigen Hepatitis." See Viral hepatitis
Autoinoculation, 93
Aversion therapy, 159

Babies, herpes and, 101, 108
Bacillary dysentery, 81
Back pain, 86
Barbiturates, 77
Beach, Dr. Frank A., 153
Behavior therapy, 159
Benign late syphilis, 17
Bishop, K. S., 143
Bladder, 34; N.S.U. and, 40; proximity to vagina of, 109; warts and, 94